English Extra

GRACE TANAKA AND KAY FERRELL

Longman

D1614107

Publisher: Mary Jane Peluso
Development Editor: Margaret Grant
Director of Production and Manufacturing: Aliza Greenblatt
Executive Managing Editor: Dominick Mosco
Electronic Production Editor: Carey Davies
Manufacturing Manager: Ray Keating

Electronic Art Production Supervisor: Ken Liao
Electronic Art Production Specialist: Steven Greydanus
Cover Design: Paul Pullara
Art Director: Merle Krumper
Interior Design: Merle Krumper, Ken Liao, Carey Davies

Illustrator: Betsy Day

INTRODUCTION

Overview

English Extra, a communicative, multiskills program of fifteen colorfully illustrated units of authentic language in context, is a comprehensive low-beginning program. *English Extra* has been designed to meet state-adopted standards nationwide, and the text addresses the SCANS (Secretary's Commission on Achieving Necessary Skills) workplace competencies for this level.

Organization of the Text

English Extra is organized around opportunities for language use in the students' own lives, beginning with the family and the home, and moving into the broader context of the town or city and the workplace. Language structures and competencies emerge from the natural environment of authentic student needs.

English Extra maintains an even pace with a steady and consistent building of skills suited to students' needs. The simplicity of the text allows the beginning learner's creativity to emerge quickly. Occasions for collaborative learning are available on nearly every page as the lessons guide students from teacher-directed learning to self-directed learning and independent language acquisition.

English Extra uses a variety of interactive opportunities to develop communicative skills. Language skills and concepts are presented in a cyclical approach (regular recycling of contexts and illustrations that introduce new communicative tasks in a familiar setting) using student-centered activities that engage and involve beginning learners, who have limited language ability. This approach provides students with functional patterns and the opportunity to expand their learning beyond patterning into authentic responses that reflect the goals of standard English.

Organization of the Unit

Each unit consists of twelve pages. The unit opener sets the stage for the theme and the vocabulary being introduced. Then, listening/reading activities teach the new vocabulary words and/or functions through colorful illustrations. Succeeding pages provide diverse practice activities (simple, direct, repetitive, each building on the one before) that give students the opportunity to work collaboratively with a partner or group to create and respond. Active research activities are provided for students and teachers to check comprehension and evaluate progress.

The second section of each unit leads students to more independent use of the language and involvement with the content, vocabulary, and functions through real-life applications: forms, surveys, graphs, receipts, shopping lists, food, job and real estate ads, school and employment applications, and phone messages. Each unit includes one or more review pages.

Beginning in Unit 6, information gap activities require students to communicate new information to their partners on such topics as prices and price tags, physical ailments, job descriptions, bank and postal services, and phone conversations.

The last page of the unit is a comprehensive summary page (a checklist of functions, vocabulary, and language forms), enabling students to see at a glance what they have learned in the unit.

Supplementary Materials

The Audio Program provides dialogues, conversations, and exercises from the text, and expansions of those exercises that are designed to help students with focused-listening and pronunciation. The Activity Book—with follow-up practice that enables students to work independently—is an integral part of the program. The Teacher's Manual gives clear instructions for presentation of the material and provides a variety of follow-up activities.

Unit	Topics	Language Functions	Listening

1

Nice to meet you.

page 1

➤ Getting acquainted
➤ In the classroom
➤ Personal information

➤ Make simple introductions.
➤ Express simple greetings.
➤ Describe feelings.
➤ Identify classroom objects.
➤ Follow simple directions.
➤ Ask for and give personal information.

➤ Hear and follow simple oral directions.
➤ Comprehend simple words in everyday context.
➤ Listen for details in introductions.
➤ Discriminate between letters.
➤ Discriminate among numbers.

2

There is no school on Saturday.

page 13

➤ Daily activities
➤ Days of the week
➤ Telling time
➤ Family relationships
➤ Home furnishings

➤ Identify and talk about daily activities.
➤ Identify and write days of the week and time expressions.
➤ Use repetition to ask for clarification.
➤ Understand appropriate expressions of leave-taking.
➤ Identify family relationships.
➤ Identify and describe location of home furnishings.

➤ Understand time expressions.
➤ Comprehend simple words in everyday context.

3

Can we buy some ice cream?

page 25

➤ Shopping in the supermarket
➤ Using money
➤ Smart shopping

➤ Introduce others.
➤ Offer assistance.
➤ Identify common foods.
➤ Ask for/give aisle location of food items in a supermarket.
➤ State likes and dislikes.
➤ Identify coins and bills and their values.
➤ Read, identify, and write money amounts.
➤ Read ads and comparison shop for food items.

➤ Listen for details in directions.
➤ Recognize spoken money amounts.
➤ Distinguish between different money amounts.

Speaking	Reading	Writing	Language Forms
➤ Make simple introductions. ➤ Express simple greetings. ➤ Pronounce letters and numbers. ➤ Ask for and give spelling of names. ➤ Ask/give personal information. ➤ Ask/answer *yes/no* and *what* questions.	➤ Discriminate among numerals and alphabet letters. ➤ Recognize basic sight words. ➤ Interpret sentences using previously practiced oral language and picture cues.	➤ Fill out simple personal information form. ➤ Write/print alphabet letters legibly. ➤ Make a graph. ➤ Write vocabulary words.	➤ Simple present tense ➤ Present continuous tense ➤ Present tense of *be* ➤ Affirmative statements ➤ *Yes/No* questions with short affirmative and negative answers ➤ *What* questions
➤ Ask/answer questions on daily activities. ➤ Ask/answer questions about the time. ➤ Ask/answer *where* questions. ➤ Describe locations. ➤ Use repetition with proper intonation to ask for clarification. ➤ Use appropriate expressions of greeting and leave-taking.	➤ Read analog and digital time. ➤ Interpret a family tree.	➤ Write previously practiced oral language. ➤ Write numerals. ➤ Fill in a grid. ➤ Label activities.	➤ Subject Pronouns ➤ Simple present tense ➤ Location *(on, next to, above, under)* ➤ Review: questions with short answers *(Yes/No, What, Where, Who)*
➤ Ask for aisle locations in the supermarket. ➤ State opinions.	➤ Read money amounts. ➤ Read simple ads. ➤ Read prices, price tags.	➤ Write/label money amounts. ➤ Generate a list.	➤ *Where* questions *(Where is/ Where are)* ➤ *I like/don't like* ➤ Offering assistance *(Can I help you?)* ➤ Review: simple present tense ➤ Review: *Yes/No* questions ➤ Review: *What is this?*

Speaking	Language Skills Reading	Writing	Language Forms
➤ Give simple directions. ➤ Practice the language of clarification. ➤ Express pleasure. ➤ Express desire.	➤ Read an expanded text. ➤ Understand and answer questions based on an expanded reading.	➤ Complete a *cloze* activity. ➤ Write brief answers (one-word or short-phrase).	➤ Location *(in, on, between, behind)* ➤ Present progressive tense *(What is ___ doing?)* ➤ *How many* questions ➤ Review: *where* questions ➤ Commands ➤ *I want* + noun ➤ Placement of adjectives
➤ Ask about another person *(How're you doing?)*. ➤ Say prices and totals. ➤ Express gratitude and emotion. ➤ Interview classmates.	➤ Read clothing ads. ➤ Read a calendar.	➤ Make a clothes shopping list. ➤ Write a date. ➤ Collect data to fill in a grid.	➤ Comparison: *larger, smaller (too large/too small)* ➤ Review: present progressive tense ➤ Polite expressions: *Can/May I help you? Let me show you...* ➤ *What (color, size)* questions ➤ *This/These* + noun
➤ Use transportation vocabulary. ➤ Give/ask for map directions. ➤ Spell names of objects with partner. ➤ Give/ask for prices. ➤ Apologize and respond to an apology.	➤ Read a map. ➤ Read map directions.	➤ Write names of objects dictated by another student. ➤ Write prices.	➤ Review: *where* questions ➤ Review: questions of time and means *(when, how)* ➤ Review: questions with *How much is/are/for ___?* ➤ Direction words *(right, left, straight)* ➤ Location *(across from, beside)*

Speaking	Reading	Writing	Language Forms
➤ Use basic emergency vocabulary on phone. ➤ Give/ask for directions. ➤ Describe the weather.	➤ Reread to identify key words. ➤ Read addresses.	➤ Write about local weather. ➤ Label body parts. ➤ Draw a map of your neighborhood.	➤ Review: present progressive tense (*What is ___ doing?*) ➤ Review: questions with *how's* ➤ Review: *Yes/No* questions ➤ Simple descriptive statements for weather (*It's raining/snowing, etc.*)
➤ Spell health vocabulary with partner. ➤ Ask for/give health information. ➤ Express sympathy and concern.	➤ Reread for specific information. ➤ Read categorized vocabulary to make appropriate responses.	➤ Complete a chart based on rereading for specific information. ➤ Spell from taped dictation.	➤ *How is/are ___?* ➤ *What is the matter with ___?* ➤ *Have/has* + noun (for illness or injury) ➤ Simple present tense of *have* ➤ Review: simple present tense (daily routine)
➤ Ask for/give information on transportation. ➤ Ask for/give advice about using community businesses and resources. ➤ Interview classmates.	➤ Read maps. ➤ Identify traffic signs. ➤ Locate places on map. ➤ Interpret a bus schedule.	➤ Construct a graph based on class surveys. ➤ Write specific times.	➤ *Let's ___.* ➤ Commands ➤ *How* questions ➤ *By ___* (transportation) ➤ Review: simple present tense

10 — Let's go have coffee.

Topics
- Occupations, job duties, and expectations
- Reading job ads
- Filling out an employment application
- Appropriate behavior in the workplace

Language Functions
- Identify occupations and occupational activities.
- Identify employment vocabulary.
- Read basic job ads.
- Fill out an employment application.
- Make a suggestion/Offer an invitation (*Let's go have coffee*).
- Express regret or decline an invitation and state a reason.
- Express necessity (*I have to…*).

Listening
- Listen for details of occupational functions.
- Comprehend language of the workplace.

11 — Dad works so hard.

Topics
- The office and factory
- Technology in the workplace
- Job responsibilities
- Safety in the workplace

Language Functions
- Ask for and give information about work.
- Use vocabulary of jobs and employment.
- Identify basic office equipment and furniture.
- Read, identify, and understand basic safety warning signs.
- Express warning or caution.
- Offer help.
- Make a request.
- Make commands.

Listening
- Listen for specific prepositions of locations.
- Follow directions for computer keyboarding.
- Comprehend terms of caution.

12 — What's the problem?

Topics
- Household problems and repairs
- Repairpersons
- The classified ads

Language Functions
- Identify and report housing repair needs.
- Identify repair people.
- Call the manager, describe the problem, and request household repairs.
- Read and compare housing ads.
- Call and ask questions about housing ads.
- Make an appointment to check on housing.
- Write a simple note requesting household repairs.

Listening
- Comprehend details of household problems.
- Understand details of a phone conversation.

Speaking	Reading	Writing	Language Forms
➤ Ask for/give information about occupations. ➤ Express regret. ➤ Decline an invitation. ➤ Express necessity.	➤ Read basic want ads. ➤ Read an employment application.	➤ Construct list of classmates' occupations. ➤ Design a job ad. ➤ Fill out an employment application.	➤ Review: questions with short answers *(Yes/No, What, Where, Who)* ➤ Simple present tense to identify occupational activities ➤ *Let's* + infinitive (suggestion) ➤ Statements expressing necessity or obligation *(I have to...)*
➤ Ask for/give information about occupations. ➤ Practice using task-related vocabulary. ➤ Give caution and safety messages. ➤ Offer help.	➤ Read basic safety warning signs. ➤ Read the computer keyboard.	➤ Fill out a personal information form. ➤ Generate responses based on context.	➤ Review: *What is this?/Is this a ___?/Where is the ___?* questions ➤ Review: present progressive tense ➤ Review: affirmative and negative commands ➤ Review: simple present tense ➤ Use verb + *ing* and verb + *s* structures appropriately.
➤ Make a phone request for repair services. ➤ Practice phone dialogue about classified ad.	➤ Read and compare classified ads. ➤ Interpret picture cues of needed repairs. ➤ Understand the note format.	➤ Write a note requesting repair services. ➤ Write a list of needed repairs.	➤ Review: present progressive tense ➤ Simple present tense to identify occupational activities ➤ Forms of politeness *(Can you...? Would you please...? Would you like...?)*

13

It's a deal!

page 145

Topics
- Renting a house
- Using the bank
- Using the post office
- Methods of payment

Language Functions
- Identify community institutions and services.
- Understand the concept of a final agreement.
- Identify and access banking services.
- Identify and access postal services.
- Fill out a money order form.
- Inquire about services.
- Request service and state need.
- Talk about and express a future event.

Listening
- Comprehend a request for service.
- Comprehend a statement of need.

14

Those kids!

page 157

Topics
- Using the telephone
- Appearances
- Generation/culture gap
- Parts of the face or facial features.

Language Functions
- Expand vocabulary through the use of synonyms and antonyms.
- Express likes and dislikes.
- Use telephone vocabulary in giving and receiving telephone messages.
- Expand and review vocabulary of body parts.
- Ask for and state opinion.
- Repeat for clarification.
- Express displeasure/complaint

Listening
- Listen to phone conversations.
- Listen to phone messages.

15

José and Carlos are having a party.

page 169

Topics
- Holidays and traditions
- Celebrations and their preparations
- Marking the calendar
- Personal preparations for a party
- Culminating activity/certificate

Language Functions
- Understand cultural concepts of housewarming, potluck, and end of school term.
- Understand the cultural concept of preparing for a party or celebration.
- Understand the significance of a certificate of completion.
- Read and mark dates on a calendar.
- Identify holidays, special dates, celebrations, and their significance.
- Identify foods from different cultures.
- Identify basic grooming habits.

Listening
- Comprehend words from other cultures (holidays, foods).

Language Skills			Language Forms
Speaking	**Reading**	**Writing**	
➤ Give directions and spell words for a partner. ➤ Practice using bank services vocabulary. ➤ Make a request for service. ➤ Make a statement of need. ➤ Inquire about services.	➤ Read addresses on letters, packages, and forms. ➤ Make inferences.	➤ Fill out a money order.	➤ Review: verbs expressing need (*I need/want...*) ➤ Review: future tense (*It'll be.../it will be...*) ➤ Review: numbers
➤ Practice phone etiquette. ➤ Ask for/state opinions. ➤ Repeat for clarification.	➤ Compare synonyms/ antonyms in context of sentences. ➤ Read phone message format.	➤ Write phone messages. ➤ Label parts of the face.	➤ Synonyms/antonyms ➤ Expressions of preference (*likes/dislikes*) ➤ *Too* + adjective ➤ Review: simple present tense (routine)
➤ Practice the language of celebrations, traditions, and holidays. ➤ Practice the language of personal success.	➤ Read multicultural terms.	➤ Make a calendar and indicate celebration dates. ➤ Make a shopping list. ➤ Complete a certificate. ➤ Write dates.	➤ Present progressive tense to express near future ➤ Review: present progressive tense ➤ Review: simple present tense ➤ Review: imperative

Acknowledgments

The authors would like to thank the following reviewers for their valuable insights and suggestions.

Peggy Armstrong
First Coast Language Consultants

Stacla S. Castaneda
Mid-City Continuing Education Center

Cathy Day
Eastern Michigan University

Carole E. M. Franklin
University of Houston

Marjorie Friedman
ELS Language Centers

Sally Gearhart
Santa Rosa Junior College

Pearl M. Gilligan
Southampton College

Charlotte Gilman
Texas Intensive English Program

Sandy B. Gittleson
Hostos Community College

John M. Kopec
Boston University

Sara McKinnon
Luong Tam Design

Kathleen B. Lund
Bristol Community College

John J. Quinn
Albany Park Community Center

Alice Savage
North Harris Montgomery Community College

Thanks to Gretchen Bitterlin and her colleagues at San Diego Community Colleges for fieldtesting the materials and providing so many excellent suggestions.

Thanks also to Carey Davies, Production Editor, and Merle Krumper, Art Director, for the lovely design and electronic production of the book.

Special thanks to friends and colleagues at Centennial Education Center and Rancho Santiago Community College District for their support of this project and their continuous friendship.

Special thanks also to Margo Grant, Development Editor, for her patience, guidance, and expertise.

And very, very special thanks to our families:

Ed, John, Stephanie, and David Tanaka
Will and Patrick Ferrell

Grace Tanaka

Kay Ferrell

Nice to meet you.

  Listen and read.

 **Practice.**

How are you?

How are you this morning?

this afternoon?

this evening?

Listen and read.

Great!   Fine!   So-so.   Good!   Happy!

Practice.

How are you today?   I'm _____.

My name is . . .

Listen and read.

Are you in my ESL class?

I'm Alicia.

It's Farrar. I'm Alicia Farrar.

Yeah! I'm José. What's your name?

What's your last name?

Practice.

My first name is Petra.
My last name is Yeltsin.
I'm Petra Yeltsin.

My first name is _____.
My last name is _____.
I'm _____.

Write.

My first name is _____.

My last name is _____.

I'm _____.

Name: _____
           first   last

How are you feeling?

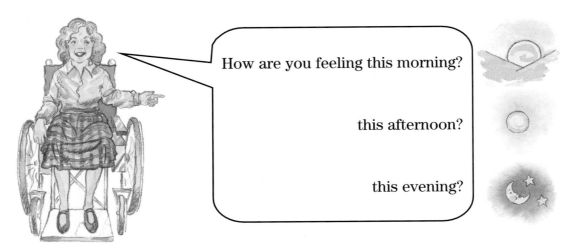

> How are you feeling this morning?
>
> this afternoon?
>
> this evening?

 Listen and read.

sad

bored

sick

angry

upset

tired

Practice.

> How're you feeling this morning?
> this afternoon?
> this evening?

> I'm sorry to hear that.

> I'm sick.

> How are you feeling _____?

> I'm _____.

> That's too bad.

Do you remember?

Read with your teacher.

A	B	C	D	E	F	G	H	I	J
K	L	M	N	O	P	Q	R	S	T
U	V	W	X	Y	Z				

a	b	c	d	e	f	g	h	i	j
k	l	m	n	o	p	q	r	s	t
u	v	w	x	y	z				

0	1	2	3	4	5	6	7	8	9
10	11	12	13	14	15	16	17	18	19
20	21	22	23	24	25	26	27	28	29
30	31	32	33	34	35	36	37	38	39
40	41	42	43	44	45	46	47	48	49
50	51	52	53	54	55	56	57	58	59
60	61	62	63	64	65	66	67	68	69
70	71	72	73	74	75	76	77	78	79
80	81	82	83	84	85	86	87	88	89
90	91	92	93	94	95	96	97	98	99
100	200	300	400	500	600	700	800	900	1000

Listen and circle the letter you hear.

1. b (v)
2. a e
3. i e

4. c s
5. g j
6. s x

7. a i
8. m n
9. y i

Listen and circle the number you hear.

1. 3 5 (13) 30
2. 2 12 20 22
3. 3 12 13 30

4. 4 6 14 24
5. 6 8 16 26
6. 9 17 19 29

7. 28 8 18 14
8. 30 13 14 3
9. 7 17 16 27

Listen and write the missing letters.

g r (e) __ t s __ u __ e n __
1 2 3 4 5 6 7 8 9 10 11 12

This is our classroom.

Listen and point.

1. board
2. calendar
3. computer
4. flag

5. map
6. clock
7. bookcase
8. projector

9. wheelchair
10. calculator
11. pencil sharpener
12. screen

Read the words with your teacher.

Is this a clock?

Listen and circle.

1.	yes	(no)	4.	yes	no	7.	yes	no	10.	yes	no
2.	yes	no	5.	yes	no	8.	yes	no	11.	yes	no
3.	yes	no	6.	yes	no	9.	yes	no	12.	yes	no

Practice.

Ask *Yes/No* Questions.

Point and ask your partner.

Is this a _____?
{ Yes, it is.
{ No, it isn't.

Practice.

Ask *What* Questions.

Point and ask your partner.

What's this?

It's a _____.

.7.
....

Here is your identification card.

Read with your teacher.

School Identification

Name: __José__   __Arroyo__
         first   last

Address: __333__   __Pico Street__
        number   street

__Duttonville__   __CA__   __92234__
     city   state   zip code

Telephone: __619__   __555-4321__
       area code   number

School Identification

Name: __Sue__   __Apple__
         first   last

Address: __142__   __Pine Street__
        number   street

__Spring Valley__   __CA__   __92234__
     city   state   zip code

Telephone: __619__   __555-9865__
       area code   number

Write your own information.

School Identification

Name: _____
        first   last

Address: _____
        number   street

_____
     city   state   zip code

Telephone: _____
       area code   number

Ask your classmates.

Ask five classmates and fill in the blanks.

What's your first name? What's your last name?

	first name	last name
1.		
2.		
3.		
4.		
5.		

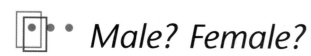

Male? Female?

Listen, read, and write.

A.

B.

C.

D.

male

female

single male
single

single female
single

_____

_____

_____

_____

E.

F.

married

divorced

_____

_____

Write about you.

Male	☐ M	Single	☐ S
Female	☐ F	Married	☐ M
		Divorced	☐ D

Print your name. _____
                        (last)   (first)

Sign your name. _____
                       (signature)

Social Security number: _____ _____ _____

SOCIAL SECURITY

504-04-3912

Barbara Brown

Count your classmates.

Number of students in class _____

single
number _____

married
number _____

divorced
number _____

✏️ **Complete the bar graph using the information above.**

	Number of students																								
	1	2	3	4	5	6	7	8	9	10	11	12	13	14	15	16	17	18	19	20	21	22	23	24	25
single number _____																									
married number _____																									
divorced number _____																									

Review.

 Listen and circle.

1. a.  ⓑ  c.

2. a.  b.  c.

3. a.  b.  c.

4. a.  b.  c.

Find the picture and write the word.

board	computer	flag	map
clock	bookcase	calculator	calendar
projector	pencil sharpener	wheelchair	screen

1. ___clock___   2. _____   3. _____   4. _____

5. _____   6. _____   7. _____   8. _____

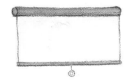   

9. _____   10. _____   11. _____   12. _____

I can do this!

_____ **Use words of greeting and introductions.**

Hello.	Hi! I'm . . .
My name is . . .	Nice to meet you.

_____ **Use words to ask and express feeling.**

How are you today?

I'm _____ .

great	fine	so-so	good	happy	
sad	bored	sick	angry	upset	tired

_____ **Express regret.**

I'm sorry to hear that.   *That's too bad.*

_____ **Identify classroom objects.**

board	bookcase	calculator	calendar
clock	computer	flag	map
pencil sharpener	projector	screen	wheelchair

_____ **Say and identify alphabet letters and numbers.**

_____ **Ask *Yes/No* questions.**

Is this a _____?   { *Yes, it is.*
                         No, it isn't.

_____ **Ask *What* questions.**

What is this? It's a _____.

_____ **Give and write personal information.**

Name: _____
                        first   last

Address: _____
                number   street   apartment number

         _____
                        city   state   zip code

Telephone: (_____) _____
              area code   number

_____ **Use contractions.**

UNIT 2

There is no school on Saturday.

Listen and read.

      Kim: Is Bic sleeping?

Charlie: Yes, he is. He needs to get up and go to work.

    May: On Saturday?

Grandpa: Wake him up! I want to go to school today.

Can Grandpa go to school on Saturday?

.13.

What do you do on Saturdays?

Read with your teacher. Circle your answer.

1. Do you shop on Saturday?
yes   no

2. Do you rest?
yes   no

3. Do you dance?
yes   no

4. Do you go to school?
yes   no

5. Do you go to work?
yes   no

6. Do you exercise?
yes   no

Practice.

Do you shop on Saturdays?

Do you _____ on Saturdays?   Yes, I do. (No, I don't.)

Look at the week.

Listen and read.

Sunday	Monday	Tuesday	Wednesday	Thursday	Friday	Saturday
S	M	T	W	Th	F	S

Today is Monday. Do you go to school on Monday?

Yes, I do. I go to school on Monday.

Today is Sunday. Do you work on Sunday?

No, I don't. I rest on Sunday.

Today is _____. Do you _____ on _____?

_____.

Practice.

1. go to school

2. rest

3. shop

4. go to work

5. dance

6. exercise

Review.

 Listen and read.

1. exercise
2. rest

3. dance
4. go to school

5. shop
6. go to work

Write the words under the pictures.

a. ____exercise____

b. _____

c. _____

d. _____

e. _____

f. _____

 Write about you.

1. I _____ on Fridays.

2. I _____ on Saturdays.

3. I _____ on Sundays.

Ask your classmates.

✏️ **Write the names of the days.**

Sunday _Sunday_   Monday _____   Tuesday _____

Wednesday _____   Thursday _____   Friday _____

Saturday _____

	S	M	T	W	Th	F	S
rest	Kay						Kay
go to work							
shop						Grace	
exercise							
dance							
go to school							

🗣️ **Ask your classmates:** *What day do you _____?*
Ask them to write their names under the day.

What day do you rest?   I rest on Saturday.

What time is it?

What time is it, Mom?

It's 7:30.

Listen and point.

It's twelve o'clock.
12:00

It's one-fifteen.
1:15

It's ten-thirty.
10:30

It's one-forty-five.
1:45

Listen and check (✔) the time you hear.

1. a. _____   b. ✔_____   2. a. _____   b. _____

3. a. _____   b. _____   4. a. _____   b. _____.

5. a. _____   b. _____   6. a. _____   b. _____

Listen and point to the picture.

1. morning

2. afternoon

3. night

A.M. = morning   P.M. = afternoon, evening, and night

Please turn on the lamp.

Listen and point.

1. lamp
2. door
3. sofa

4. calendar
5. rug
6. floor

7. picture
8. wall
9. television

10. chair
11. table
12. window

Practice. Point and ask your partner *Where* questions.

Where is the _____?

It's $\begin{cases} \text{on} \\ \text{next to} \\ \text{above} \\ \text{under} \end{cases}$ the _____.

The book is **on** the table.

The student is **next to** the teacher.

The clock is **above** the board.

The pencil is **under** the book.

This is the Castro family.

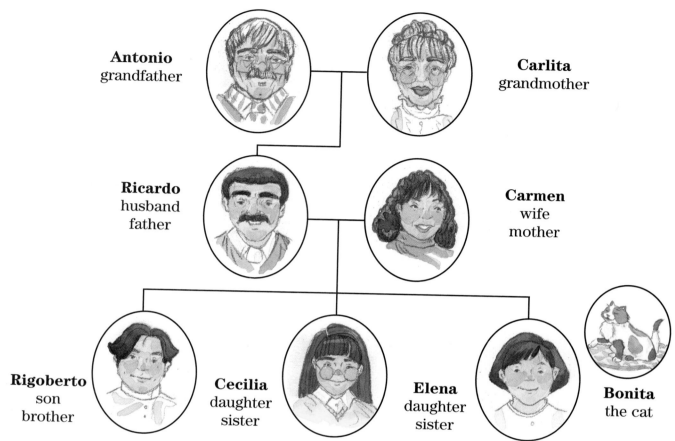

Antonio
grandfather

Carlita
grandmother

Ricardo
husband
father

Carmen
wife
mother

Rigoberto
son
brother

Cecilia
daughter
sister

Elena
daughter
sister

Bonita
the cat

Listen and read.

The Castro Family

Meet the Castro family. Here are grandfather and grandmother. They have one son. His wife is Carmen. Carmen and her husband have one son and two daughters. Who is Bonita?

Read and draw a line.

1. Ricardo's wife
2. Carmen's husband
3. Ricardo's son
4. Carmen's daughter
5. grandmother
6. grandfather
7. cat
8. Cecilia's sister

a. Cecilia
b. Rigoberto
c. Carlita
d. Carmen
e. Bonita
f. Ricardo
g. Antonio
h. Elena

I'm her brother. She's my sister.

✎ **Read and write.**

1. I'm her daughter. She's my _mother_ .

Carmen   Elena

2. I'm her father. She's my _____ .

Cecilia   Ricardo

3. I'm her daughter. She's my _____ .

Cecilia   Carmen

4. I'm her husband. She's my _____ .

Ricardo   Carmen

5. I'm her brother. She's my _____ .

Rigoberto   Cecilia

6. He's my father. I'm his _____ .

Rigoberto   Ricardo

✎ **Write and tell about your family.**

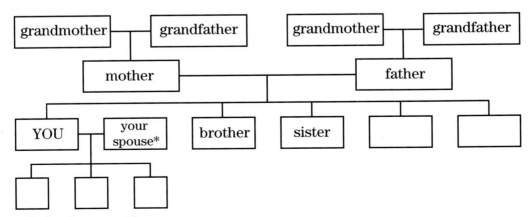

* spouse = your husband or your wife

Review.

Listen, then circle or make an X.

1. Make an X on the grandmother.
2. Circle the fathers.
3. Place an X on each sister.
4. Circle the mothers.

Write the letter.

1. Who is the sister?   *f*
2. Who is the grandfather?   _____
3. Who is the son?   _____
4. Who is the husband of A?   _____
5. Who is the wife of B?   _____
6. Who are the daughters?   _____

Write the word.

I	He	She	It	You	We	They

1. The grandmother is happy. _She_ is from Cuba.
2. The daughters are sick today. _____ are feeling sad.
3. The Castros live in Spring Valley. _____ work and go to school.
4. The cat is fat. _____ is hungry.

It's time to go.

It's time to go!

Listen and read.

Bic: Good morning! It's time to go. Where are my keys?
Kim: Are they next to the television?
Charlie: No, I don't see them. Are they under the chair?
Kim: There they are, under the table.
Bic: Oh! I see them now. Goodbye, Grandpa. See you later.

Listen and write the words.

Good __*morning*__. It's _____ to go.

Where are my _____?

Are they next to the _____?

No, I don't _____ _____.

Are they _____ the chair?

There they are, _____ the _____.

Oh! I _____ them now. _____, Grandpa. See you _____.

I can do this!

____ **Identify and talk about some daily activities.**

| shop | rest | dance | exercise | go to work | go to school |

____ **Ask for, say, and write the time. (Morning, afternoon, and night.)**

____ **Identify and write the days of the week.**

Sunday	Monday	Tuesday	Wednesday
Thursday	Friday	Saturday	

____ **Identify, ask, and talk about family relationships.**

grandfather	grandmother	father	mother
husband	wife	son	daughter
brother	sister	children	spouse

____ **Identify items in the living room.**

chair	sofa	floor	calendar	lamp	door
window	table	rug	wall	television	picture

____ **Ask for and describe the location of furniture in the living room.**

____ **Use repetition with proper intonation to ask for clarification.**
On Saturday?

____ **Understand the appropriate expressions of greeting and leave-taking.**

| Good morning. | See you later. | Goodbye. | Good night. |

____ **Understand and use subject pronouns.**

| I | he | she | it | you | we | they |

____ **Use question structures with appropriate short answers.**

Yes/No	*Is Bic sleeping?*	*Yes, he is. (No, he isn't.)*
	Do you exercise?	*Yes, I do. (No, I don't.)*
What	*What is on the table?*	
Where	*Where is the lamp?*	*It's _____.*
Who	*Who is Carmen?*	*She is _____.*

UNIT 3

Can we buy some ice cream?

Listen.

Sue: Hello, José. This is my husband, Ken, and my daughter, Kathy. Ken, José is a student at our school.

José: Good morning! Welcome to our store!

Ken: Nice to meet you, José. Do you work here every Saturday?

José: Yes, Saturdays, Sundays, and holidays, too.

Kathy: Where's the ice cream? Can we buy some ice cream, Mom?

Listen again and read.

Where's the ice cream?

 Listen and read.

José: Can I help you?
Sue: Yes. Where's the ice cream?
José: It's in aisle 2 with the frozen foods.
Sue: Aisle 2?
José: Yes. Over there.
Sue: Thank you.
Kathy: I love ice cream!

 Listen, find the picture, and read the word.

1. cake

2. bread

3. rice

4. pasta

5. flour

6. coffee

7. tea

8. soda

9. salt

10. sugar

11. fish

12. beef

13. pork

14. chicken

15. cabbage

16. broccoli

17. juice

18. ice cream

19. milk

20. butter

Where are the oranges?

Listen, read, and practice with your partner.

José: Can I help you?
Ken: Yes. Where are the oranges?
José: They're in aisle 1 with the apples.
Ken: Aisle 1?
José: Yes. Over there.
Ken: Thank you.
Kathy: I love oranges!

1. Fruits	Vegetables
oranges	beans
apples	cabbage
bananas	carrots
peaches	broccoli
	potatoes

2. Frozen foods
ice cream
juice

3. Baking Goods
flour
sugar
salt

4. Meats, Poultry, Fish
chicken
beef
fish
pork

5. Dairy Products
milk
butter

6. Rice/ Noodles
rice
noodles
pasta

7. Beverages
soda
coffee
tea

8. Bakery
cake
cookies
bread

Listen and read the food words.

1. cookies

2. noodles

3. oranges

4. peaches

5. bananas

6. potatoes

7. beans

8. carrots

9. sodas

10. chickens

Write the foods you like and the ones you don't like. Use the words above.

I like _____, _____, and _____, but

I don't like _____ and _____ very much.

Review.

  Listen and circle the words you hear.

1.   a.   b.   c.

2.   a.   b.   c.

3.   a.   b.   c.

4.   a.   b.   c.

5.   a.   b.   c.

Review.

  Listen, look at the picture, and circle *Yes* or *No*.

1. (Yes)   No   **2.** Yes   No   **3.** Yes   No   **4.** Yes   No

5. Yes   No   **6.** Yes   No   **7.** Yes   No   **8.** Yes   No

9. Yes   No   **10.** Yes   No   **11.** Yes   No   **12.** Yes   No

Practice *Yes/No* questions.

Point and ask: Is this _____?   { Yes, it is.
                                                No, it isn't.

Practice *What* questions.

Point and ask: What is this?   It's _____.

Do you sell soda?

Do you sell _____? Yes, we do. (No, we don't.)

Ask *Yes/No* questions. Do you sell _____?

1. bananas	11. calculators	21. flags	31. pork
2. beans	12. calendars	22. ice cream	32. potatoes
3. beef	13. carrots	23. keys	33. rice
4. bookcases	14. chairs	24. lamps	34. rugs
5. books	15. chicken	25. maps	35. salt
6. bread	16. clocks	26. noodles	36. sodas
7. broccoli	17. coffee	27. peaches	37. sofas
8. butter	18. computers	28. pencils	38. sugar
9. cabbages	19. cookies	29. pens	39. tea
10. cakes	20. fish	30. pictures	40. televisions

Write some other things you can buy at the supermarket.

_____   _____

_____   _____

Write some things you can't buy at the supermarket.

_____   _____

_____   _____

I like cookies! I like cake!

What do you like?

apples	butter	cookies	oranges	salt
bananas	cabbage	fish	peaches	soda
beef	cake	ice cream	pork	sugar
beans	carrots	juice	potatoes	tea
bread	chicken	milk	pasta	
broccoli	coffee	noodles	rice	

✎ **Look at the food words and write a list.**

I like _____   I don't like _____

_____   _____

_____   _____

_____   _____

_____   _____

🗣🗣✎ **Work with a partner and compare your lists. Write new lists.**

We like _____   We don't like _____

_____   _____

_____   _____

"I'm Going to the Market" Game.

Teacher: I'm going to the market, and I'm going to buy cookies.
Student 1: I'm going to the market, and I'm going to buy cookies and apples.
Student 2: I'm going to the market, and I'm going to buy cookies, apples, and tea . . .

(Each new student repeats the food already selected and adds another food item.)

How much does it cost?

 Listen and point.

a penny   a nickel   a dime   a quarter   a half dollar

a one-dollar bill   a five-dollar bill

a ten-dollar bill   a twenty-dollar bill

 Look at the money and write the amount.

1. _____a dime_____   2. _____   3. _____

4. _____   5. _____   6. _____

7. _____   8. _____   9. _____

How much money do you have?

a penny

a nickel

a dime

a quarter

a half dollar

a one-dollar bill

a five-dollar bill

a ten-dollar bill

a twenty-dollar bill

Listen and circle the amount you hear.

1. a. $2.75   b. ($12.75)   c. $3.75   5. a. $4.85   b. $14.85   c. $3.75

2. a. $2.10   b. $5.10   c. $10.10   6. a. $25.42   b. $25.43   c. $25.44

3. a. $50.73   b. $15.73   c. $14.73   7. a. $15.00   b. $50.00   c. $55.00

4. a. $7.00   b. $700.00   c. $17.00   8. a. $1.15   b. $15.00   c. $1.50

Listen and write the amount you hear.

1. ___$15.42___   6. _____

2. _____   7. _____

3. _____   8. _____

4. _____   9. _____

5. _____   10. _____

Count the money in your pocket. How much do you have? _____

Which is the best buy?

We have a great buy on peaches today.

✎ **Which is the best buy? Circle the answer.**

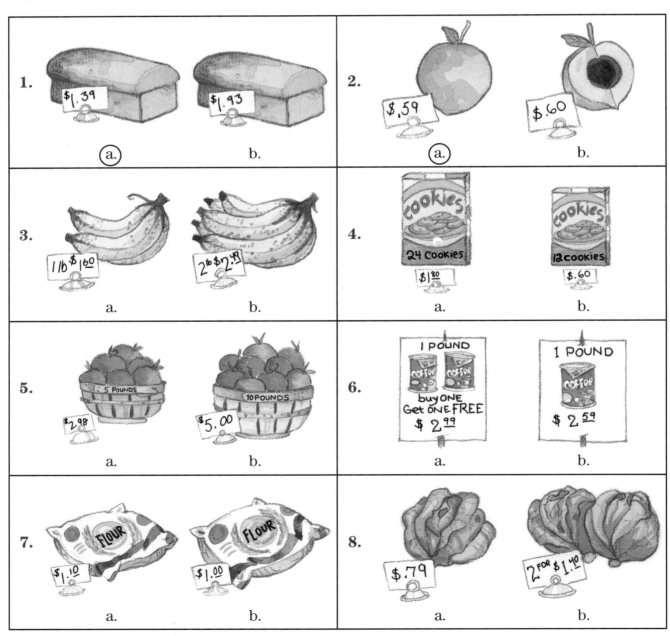

1. a. ($1.39) b. ($1.93)
   (a.) circled

2. a. ($.59) b. ($.60)
   (a.) circled

3. a. (1 lb $1.60) b. (2 lb $2.49)

4. a. (24 cookies $1.80) b. (12 cookies $.60)

5. a. (5 pounds $2.98) b. (10 pounds $5.00)

6. a. (buy ONE Get ONE FREE $2.99) b. (1 POUND $2.59)

7. a. ($1.10) b. ($1.00)

8. a. ($.79) b. (2 FOR $1.40)

Review.

Listen and circle the amount you hear.

1. 2.

3. 4.

Circle the amount you hear.

1. a. $ 5.95 (b.) $2.95 c. $3.95	**2.** a. $ 1.25 b. $1.29 c. $1.01
3. a. $ 2.49 b. $1.49 c. $3.49	**4.** a. $ 1.15 b. $1.50 c. $1.51
5. a. $ 3.25 b. $3.15 c. $ .95	**6.** a. $ 6.95 b. $ .69 c. $9.60

Circle the best buy.

1.
   6 for $6.00   12 for $10.95
      a.   b.

2.
   4 lbs. for $8.00   8 lbs. for $12.00
      a.   b.

3.
   3 for $1.00   12 for $5.00
      a.   b.

4.
   6-pack for $1.79 $ .55
      a.   b.

I can do this!

_____ **Introduce others.**
This is my husband, Ken, and my daughter, Kathy.

_____ **Offer assistance.**
Can I help you?

_____ **Identify common food items.**

cabbage	carrots	broccoli	potatoes	peaches
cake	cookies	bread	rice	pasta
noodles	soda	coffee	tea	flour
oranges	apples	bananas	milk	beans
salt	chicken	beef	fish	pork

_____ **Ask for and give aisle location of food items in a supermarket.**
Where is the _____?   It's in aisle _____.
Where are the _____s?   They're in aisle _____.

_____ **State likes and dislikes.**
I like _____.   I don't like _____.
We like _____.   We don't like _____.

_____ **Identify coins and bills and their values.**
penny   nickel   dime   quarter   half dollar
a one-dollar bill   a five-dollar bill
a ten-dollar bill   a twenty-dollar bill

_____ **Read, identify, and write money amounts.**

_____ **Read ads and comparison shop for food items.**

_____ **Understand the concept of "best buy."**

Home again, home again.

Listen and read.

curtains

refrigerator

shelf

microwave

sink

stove

cabinet

Between. The sink is between the stove and the refrigerator.

The Apple family has a big kitchen. The sink is between the <u>stove</u> and the <u>refrigerator</u>. There is a <u>microwave</u> above the stove and a <u>cabinet</u> under the sink. There is another cabinet next to the refrigerator. A <u>shelf</u> is above that cabinet. The <u>sink</u> is under the window, and there are <u>curtains</u> on the window.

Write the missing words.

The Apple family has a big kitchen. The sink is between the ___*stove*___ and

the _____. There is a _____ above the stove and a

_____ under the sink. There is another cabinet next to the refrigerator.

A _____ is above that cabinet. The _____ is under the window,

and there are _____ on the window.

They're unpacking the groceries.

Listen and read.

Practice.

bread	cookies	soda	fish
bananas	oranges	rice	coffee
potatoes	carrots	salt	tea
chicken	cabbage		

on the table	in the refrigerator
on the shelf	in the cabinet
in the sink	in the cabinet under the sink

Want some help?

Listen and read.

Listen and read.

The Said family is cleaning house. Ali is washing the clothes. Farima is sweeping the floor. Someone is cleaning the upstairs bathroom. A young boy is hanging out the clothes. Who's reading a book?

What are the rooms in the house?

Behind. The yard is behind the house.

Listen and read.

The Said family lives in a four-bedroom house. The bedrooms are all upstairs. There are two bathrooms. The dining room is downstairs between the living room and the kitchen. The laundry room is in the basement. The garage is next to the kitchen. The yard is behind the house.

Write the missing words.

1. What rooms are in the house? The ___bedrooms___, _____, _____, _____, and _____ are rooms in the Said house.

2. How many bedrooms are in the house? There are _____ bedrooms.

3. How many bathrooms are in the house? There are _____ bathrooms.

4. Where is the laundry room? It is in the _____.

5. Where is the yard? It's _____ the house.

6. Where is the garage? It's _____ to the _____.

Who's doing what? Where?

Look at the picture and write the words.

basement	bathroom	bedroom	dining room	garage
kitchen	laundry room	living room	yard	

1. ___bedroom___   4. _____   7. _____

2. _____   5. _____   8. _____

3. _____   6. _____   9. _____

Listen and read.

Ali is washing the clothes. Grandpa is reading a book in his bedroom. Farima is sweeping the downstairs bathroom floor, and her brother is cleaning the upstairs bathtub. Linda is making her bed, and Mohammed is cleaning his bedroom. Grandma is cooking in the kitchen. Ibrahim is cutting the grass in the yard, and Frank is hanging out the clothes.

Practice.

Practice.

Where is Grandma Said?

She's in the kitchen.

Where is/are _____?

    Farima and her brother

    Ali

    Grandpa Said

    Linda

    Grandma Said

    Mohammed

    Ibrahim

    Frank

She/He is in the _____.

They are in the _____.

    bedroom

    bathrooms

    kitchen

    laundry room

    garage

    yard

    dining room

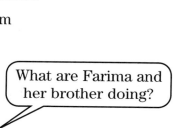

What are Farima and her brother doing?

They're cleaning the bathrooms.

What is/are _____ doing?

    Grandpa

    Linda

    Grandma

    Mohammed

    Ibrahim

    Farima

    Ali

    Frank

    Farima and her brother

He's/She's _____.

They're _____.

    reading a book

    sweeping the bathroom floor

    making the bed

    cooking in the kitchen

    cutting the grass

    cleaning the bedroom

    washing the clothes

    hanging out the clothes

    cleaning the bathtub

José's place.

Here's where I live.
This is my place.

Listen and read.

This is my apartment. It's a one-bedroom apartment. It has a bedroom, a living room, a kitchen, and a bathroom. In my bedroom, I have a bed, two night stands, two lamps, a dresser with a mirror, and a closet where I hang my clothes. I have a toilet, a shower, and a tub in the bathroom. What do you see in my living room?

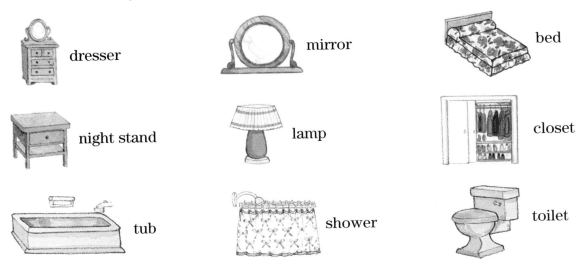

dresser

mirror

bed

night stand

lamp

closet

tub

shower

toilet

Review.

Listen and write the word.

sofa	sink	toilet	cabinet
shower	dresser	microwave	refrigerator
lamp	stove	tub	bed
table	picture	television	night stand

Living room

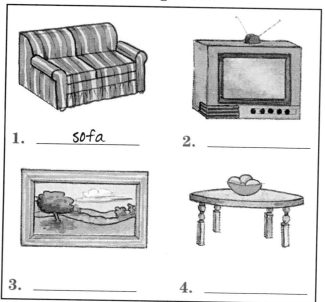

1. sofa   2. _____

3. _____   4. _____

Kitchen

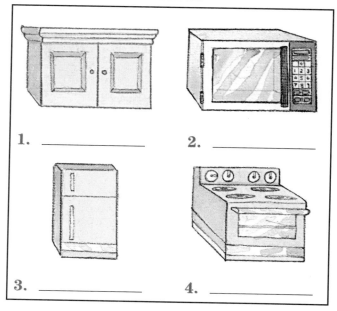

1. _____   2. _____

3. _____   4. _____

Bedroom

1. _____   2. _____

3. _____   4. _____

Bathroom

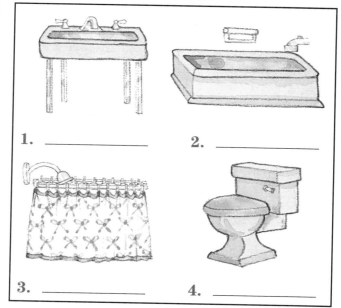

1. _____   2. _____

3. _____   4. _____

Today is Carmen's birthday.

✏️ **Read and answer.**

Today is Carmen's birthday. She's 35 years old. The Castro family is getting ready for her birthday party. Her daughters are cleaning all the rooms. Her husband and her son are hanging balloons. Her mother is cooking food for the party.

1. Who's having a birthday party?   _____

2. What are Carmen's daughters doing?   _____

3. Who's cooking the food?   _____

4. How old is Carmen today?   _____

5. What are her husband and son doing?   _____

Balloons, balloons, balloons.

Here are the balloons for the party.

How many red balloons do you want?

I want 5 red balloons.

| red | yellow | blue | green | purple | orange |

✏️ **Write.**

1. How many green balloons do you want?

I want _4_ _green_ balloons.

2. How many blue balloons do you want?

I want _____ balloons.

3. How many purple balloons do you want?

I want _____ balloons.

4. How many orange balloons do you want?

I want _____ balloons.

5. How many yellow balloons do you want?

I want _____ balloons.

6. How many red balloons do you want?

I want _____ balloons.

Counting the cookies.

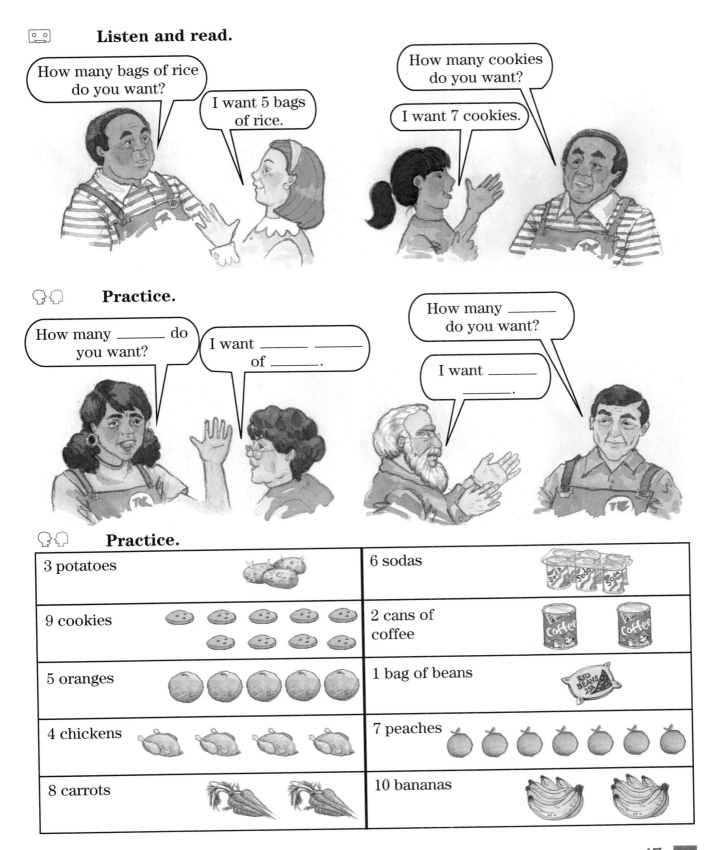

How many bags of rice do you want?

I want 5 bags of rice.

How many cookies do you want?

I want 7 cookies.

Practice.

How many _____ do you want?

I want _____ _____ of _____.

How many _____ do you want?

I want _____ _____.

Practice.

3 potatoes		6 sodas	
9 cookies		2 cans of coffee	
5 oranges		1 bag of beans	
4 chickens		7 peaches	
8 carrots		10 bananas	

I can do this!

____ **Ask and give location of objects.**

on the shelf	behind the house	under the shelf
in the sink	above the stove	between the stove and the refrigerator

____ **Identify and find the rooms of a house.**

bathroom	bedroom	dining room	living room
kitchen	yard	garage	laundry room

____ **Identify and find items in the house.**

bed	closet	mirror	sink	night stand
cabinet	curtain	picture	stove	microwave
toilet	shower	dresser	tub	refrigerator

____ **Identify and talk about some common household cleaning activities.**

wash clothes	sweep the floor	make the bed
clean the bathroom	cut the grass	hang out the laundry

____ **Identify colors.**

red	yellow	blue	green	orange	purple

____ **Ask and answer questions of where people are and what they are doing.**

____ **Ask for clarification.**
Huh? What?

____ **Ask questions with *How many*.**

____ **Express pleasure.**
Terrific!

____ **Express desire.**
I want . . .   I'd love . . . .

UNIT 5

Shop 'til you drop!

Listen and read.

Dutton's Department Store

Hello, Makeba.

Nice to see you, too. Can I help you? Are you looking for something special?

Let me show you some sweaters. What size does she wear?

Hi, Petra. It's nice to see you today.

Yes, I need a gift for Carmen Castro. Today is her birthday.

Listen and read.

Makeba is shopping for a gift for Carmen's birthday. Petra is working at the department store. She's helping Makeba. Farima is shopping, too. She's buying socks for her son. Hiroshi Tanaka is in the Men's Clothes Department, and he's buying a suit.

Listen and write.

1. Makeba is shopping for a _____gift_____ for Carmen's birthday.
2. Petra is _____ at the department _____.
3. Petra is _____ Makeba.
4. Farima is buying _____ for her _____.
5. Hiroshi is buying a new _____.

More shopping.

Dutton's Department Store

Men's Clothes

Women's Clothes   Children's Clothes   Housewares

Listen and read.

Petra and Makeba are in the Women's Clothes Department. Farima and her son are in the Children's Clothes Department. Hiroshi and a salesperson are in the Men's Clothes Department. Who is in the Housewares Department?

Listen and write the missing words.

1. Petra is in the ___Women's___ Clothes ___Department___.

2. Farima and her _____ are in the _____.

3. Where is Hiroshi? He's _____.

4. How many people are in Dutton's Department Store? There are _____ people in the department store.

What color is the coat?

Look, listen, and point.

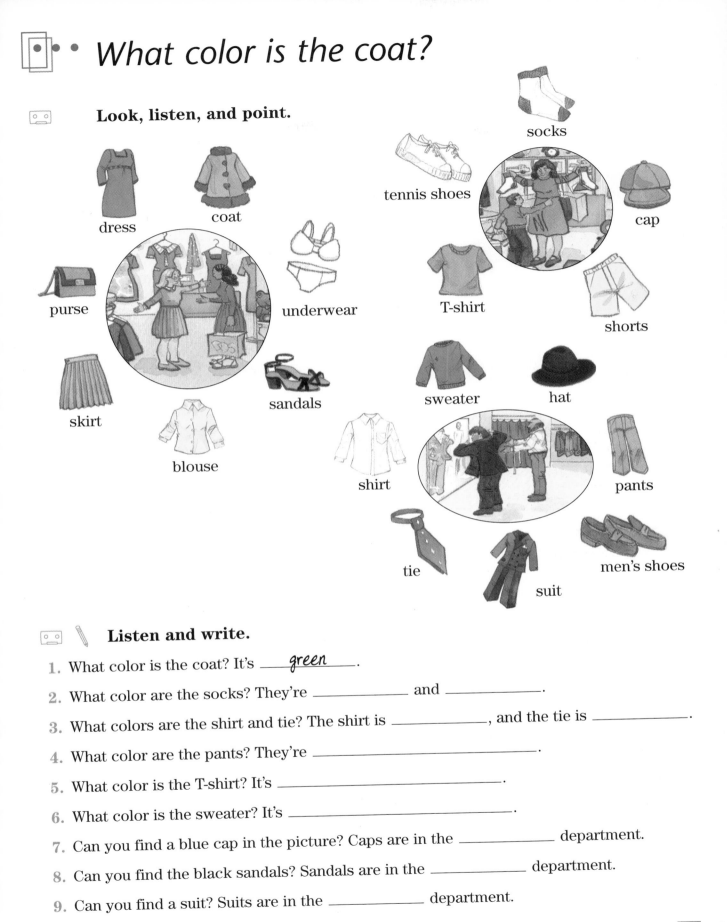

dress

coat

socks

tennis shoes

cap

purse

underwear

T-shirt

shorts

sweater

hat

skirt

sandals

blouse

shirt

pants

tie

men's shoes

suit

Listen and write.

1. What color is the coat? It's ___green___.

2. What color are the socks? They're _____ and _____.

3. What colors are the shirt and tie? The shirt is _____, and the tie is _____.

4. What color are the pants? They're _____.

5. What color is the T-shirt? It's _____.

6. What color is the sweater? It's _____.

7. Can you find a blue cap in the picture? Caps are in the _____ department.

8. Can you find the black sandals? Sandals are in the _____ department.

9. Can you find a suit? Suits are in the _____ department.

Small, medium, and large.

May I help you?

What size do you need?

What color?

Yes, I'm looking for a T-shirt.

Medium.

Orange.

S Small

M Medium

L Large

Practice.

May I help you?

What size?

What color?

Yes, I'm looking for
_____.

Exchange with your partner.

Can you tell me what you're wearing?

Practice.

> Can you tell me what you're wearing?

> I'm wearing a ___red___ ___shirt___ and ___blue___ ___pants___.

You

Your Classmate

Ask your classmates. Then count the students who are wearing the same color clothes. Write the number in the chart.

	black	red	yellow	orange	blue	green	brown	white	gray
shirts									
blouses									
pants									
dresses									
shorts									
shoes									
sandals									
sweaters									
socks									
coats									

Let's go shopping.

Read the ads.

You have
$100.00!

What do you
want to buy?

Make a shopping list.

My Shopping List

Item	Number	Cost

Total _____

Party! Party! Party!

Listen and read.

Bic Ly: Happy birthday, Carmen.
Hiroshi: Yeah! Happy birthday from me, too.
Carmen: Great to see you guys. I'm glad you're here.
We have lots of food and soda. Help yourself.
Turn on the music. Let's dance!

Answer the questions.

1. Who is having a party? _____

2. Who is at the party? _____

3. What are they doing? _____

4. When is Carmen's birthday? _____

Find your birthday.

Read with your teacher.

January	July
February	August
March	September
April	October
May	November
June	December

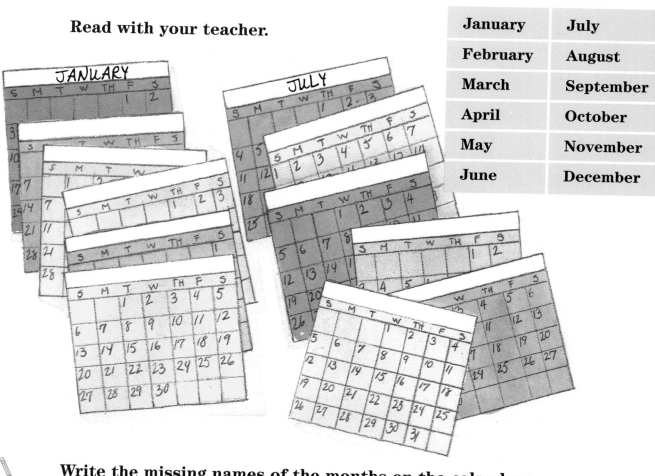

Write the missing names of the months on the calendars.

Can you find your birthday? Circle the month.

Write.

What month is your birthday? _____

What date is it? _____

My birthday is on _____ _____.
                                  month   date

Talk to three classmates. Write their names and their birthdays.

Happy Birthday to You!

Name	Month	Day
_____	_____	_____
_____	_____	_____
_____	_____	_____

I'm so happy!

Listen and read.

Happy birthday!
How're you doing?

Gee, thanks.
I'm so happy.

Here's a gift for you.

Oh! Can I open it now?

Sure. Please do.

I hope you like it.

You're welcome.

Oh! A book!
I do. Thank you very much.

surprised

excited

thrilled

Practice with your classmate.

Happy birthday!
How're you doing?
Here's a gift for you.
Sure. Please do.
I hope you like it.
You're welcome.

Gee, thanks.
I'm so _____.
Oh! Can I open it now?
Oh! ___ _____.
I do. Thank you very much.

a camera   a sweater   a wallet

an umbrella   a watch   a purse

57

Too small? Too large?

This sweater is too **small**.

Yes. Do you have one?

Do you want a **larger** size?

Let's look.

This cap is too **large**.

Yes. Do you have one?

Do you want a **smaller** size?

Let's look.

Practice.

This/these _____ is/are too _____.

Yes. Do you have one?

Do you want a _____ size?

Let's look.

1.

2.

3.

4.

5.

6.

7.

8.

Review.

Listen and circle the same amount.

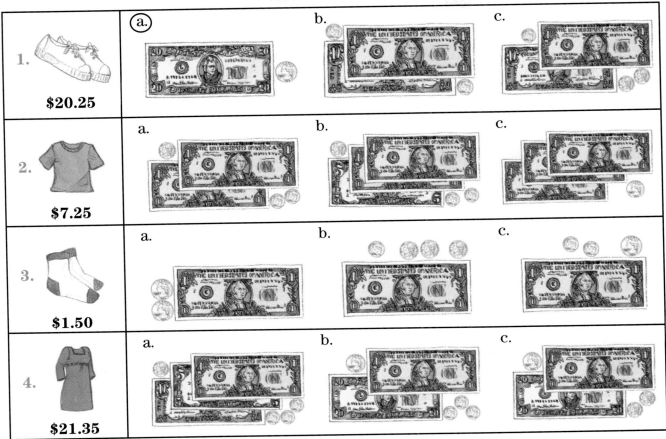

	a.	b.	c.
1. $20.25	(a.)		
2. $7.25			
3. $1.50			
4. $21.35			

Listen and make a ✔ on the amount you hear.

1.	a. $15.15 ✔	b. $7.25	c. $50.15
2.	a. $20.26	b. $40.26	c. $4.26
3.	a. $13.30	b. $30.13	c. $33.13
4.	a. $17.67	b. $70.67	c. $67.17

I can do this!

____ **Offer assistance.**
Can I help you? Let me show you.

____ **Identify and describe articles of clothing by color and size.**

dress	purse	underwear	coat
blouse	skirt	sandals	T-shirt
socks	cap	hat	shorts
men's shoes	sweater	shirt	tie
tennis shoes	pants	suit	

____ **Identify different departments in a department store.**

____ **Identify clothing sizes.**

small S	medium M	large L

____ **Shop for clothing items and ask to exchange them.**

____ **Read clothing ads and comparison shop.**

____ **Listen for and say prices and totals.**

____ **Describe and discuss a birthday celebration.**

____ **Read a calendar.**

____ **Ask for, say, and write dates.**

____ **Express gratitude.**
Thank you.   Gee, thanks.

____ **Use words of emotion.**
surprised   excited   thrilled   happy

We're having a yard sale. Can you come?

Listen and read.

Hello, Van, we're having a yard sale tomorrow. Can you come?

It's at the community center near my church. Here's a map.

Meet me at nine o'clock.

So long. See you tomorrow.

Maybe. Where is it?

Oh, good! What time?

Okay. See you at nine tomorrow. Goodbye!

• • • • • • • • • • • • • • • • • • •

Answer the questions.

1. Where are José and Van going? _____

2. When are they going? _____

3. What time are they going? _____

Practice. Ask your classmate.

How is Van Ly going?

by bicycle?

by car?

by bus?

by subway?

on foot?

Look at José's map.

Listen and find the place on the map.

1. school
2. park
3. market

4. post office
5. church
6. bus stop

7. movie theater
8. bank

left

right

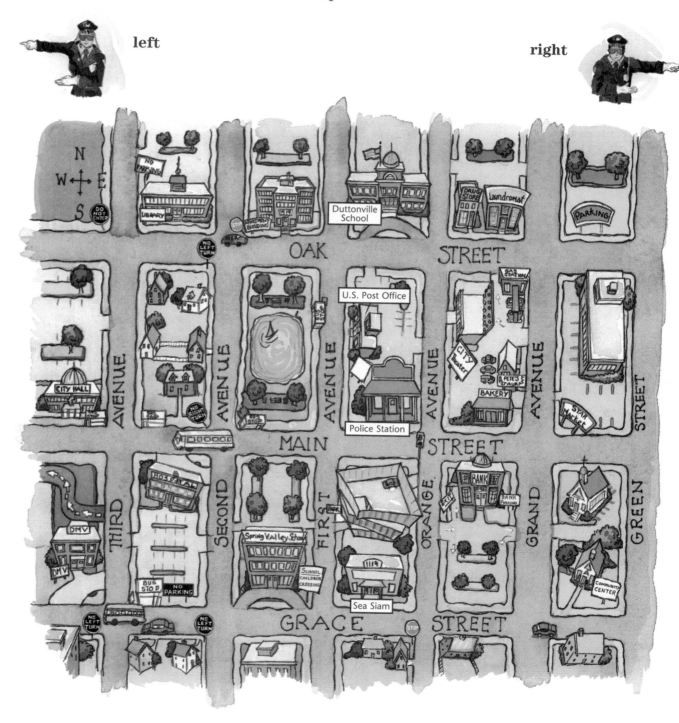

How can I get from Duttonville School to the park?

Look, listen, and read.

walk

go straight

go left

go right

beside

across from

on the corner

between

How can I get from school to the park?

Turn right. Go to First Avenue. It's between First Avenue and Second Avenue.

How can I get from the movie theater to the Sea Siam Restaurant?

Go left to Orange Avenue. Go straight. It's on Grace Street between Orange and First Street.

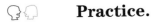

Practice.

How can I get from . . .

1. the post office to the bank?
2. the market to Duttonville School?
3. the corner of Second Avenue and Oak Street to the movie theater?
4. the market to the post office?
5. the library to City Hall?
6. the post office to the bus stop on the corner of Main and Second Avenue?

Glad to see you!

Listen and read.

Answer the questions.

1. Where are Grandpa and José? _____

2. What are they doing? _____

3. Where do *you* go to yard sales? _____

Pots and pans.

Yard Sale

Appliances - $1.00 to $25.00
Pots and Pans - $.10 to $2.00
Clothing - $.50 to $5.00

Look, listen, and write the number in the circle.

1. broom
2. coffee pot
3. dishes
4. dryer

5. glasses
6. iron
7. ironing board
8. pots and pans

9. tea kettle
10. ties
11. toaster
12. trash can

13. vacuum
14. washer

Review.

Yard Sale
Appliances - $1.00 to $25.00
Pots and Pans - $.10 to $2.00
Clothing - $.50 to $5.00

SALE

Listen and write the letter on the line.

1. _N_
2. _____
3. _____

4. _____
5. _____
6. _____

7. _____
8. _____
9. _____

Ask your partner.

Ask your partner to find the picture.
Spell the word for your partner to write.

Find the vacuum. v-a-c-u-u-m

I'm writing vacuum under the picture.

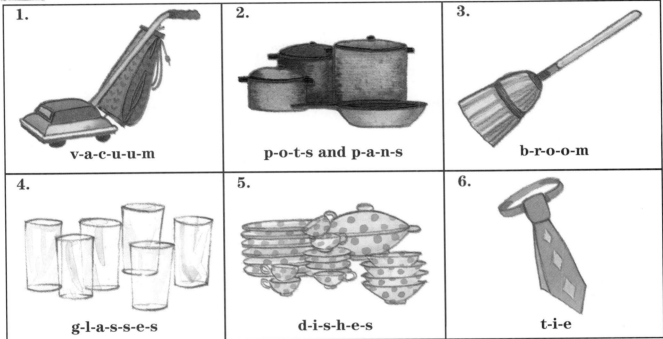

1. v-a-c-u-u-m

2. p-o-t-s and p-a-n-s

3. b-r-o-o-m

4. g-l-a-s-s-e-s

5. d-i-s-h-e-s

6. t-i-e

Listen to your partner.
Find the picture and write the word on the line.

a.

b.

c.

d. *tea kettle*

e.

f.

Ask your partner. Student B

**Ask your partner to find the picture.
Spell the word for your partner to write.**

Find the tea kettle. t-e-a k-e-t-t-l-e

I'm writing tea kettle under the picture.

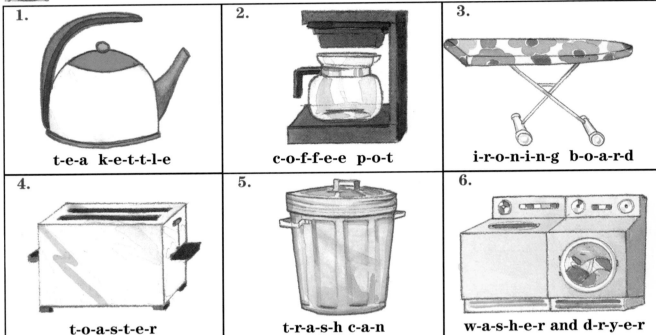

1.

t-e-a k-e-t-t-l-e

2.

c-o-f-f-e-e p-o-t

3.

i-r-o-n-i-n-g b-o-a-r-d

4.

t-o-a-s-t-e-r

5.

t-r-a-s-h c-a-n

6.

w-a-s-h-e-r and d-r-y-e-r

**Listen to your partner.
Find the picture and write the word on the line.**

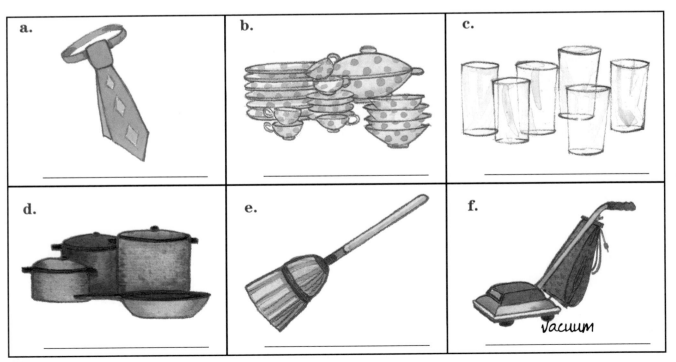

a.

_____

b.

_____

c.

_____

d.

_____

e.

_____

f.

vacuum

_____

Ask your partner.

  Ask your partner for the price. Write it on the line.

 How much for the ___coffee pot___ ?    $ 1.50 .

1. ___$ 1.50___

2. _____ ○ $5.25

3. _____

4. _____ ○ $3.00

5. _____

6. _____ ○ $2.25

7. _____

8. _____

9. _____

10. _____

11. _____ ○ $.75

12. _____ ○ $25.00

13. _____ ○ $25.00

14. _____

15. _____ 10 for $1.00

16. _____ ○ $15.00

17. _____ $.05 each

18. _____ $3.00 for set

19. _____

20. _____

•• *Ask your partner* **Student B**

✏ **Ask your partner for the price. Write it on the line.**

How much for the ___chair___ ? $5.25.

1.
○ $1.50

2. $5.25

3.
○ $1.25

4. _____

5.
○ $12.00

6. _____

7.
○ $1.80

8.
○ 3 for $1.00

9.
○ $.90

10.
○ 10 for $6.00

11. _____

12. _____

13. _____

14.
○ $.25 each

15. _____

16. _____

17. _____

18. _____

19.
○ $2.25

20.
○ $1.25

Let's figure it out!

How much is the pencil? It's $.05.

How much are the pencils? They're $.15.

Student A: Ask your partner for the price.

Student B: Ask your partner for the price.

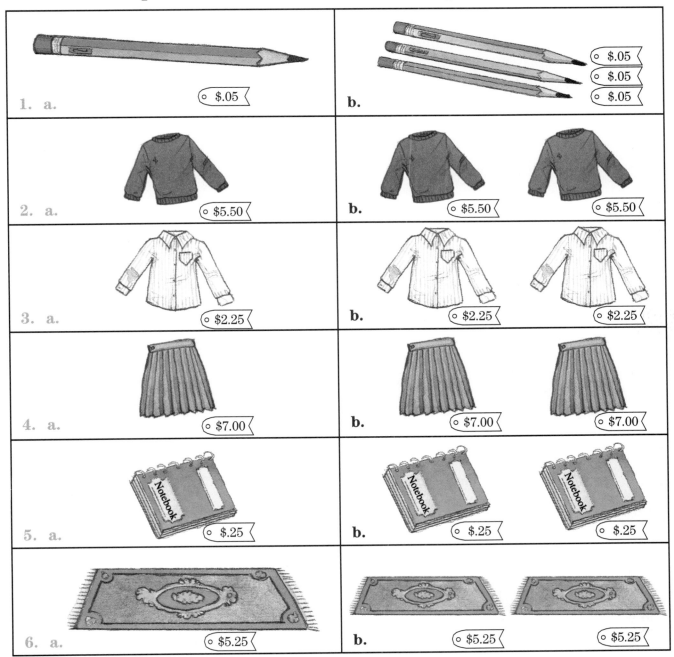

1. a. $.05

    b. $.05 $.05 $.05

2. a. $5.50

    b. $5.50 $5.50

3. a. $2.25

    b. $2.25 $2.25

4. a. $7.00

    b. $7.00 $7.00

5. a. $.25

    b. $.25 $.25

6. a. $5.25

    b. $5.25 $5.25

I can do this!

_____ **Understand and discuss the concept of a yard/garage sale.**

_____ **Extend an invitation and make a plan.**
Can you come to the _____?   Meet me at _____.

_____ **Read and interpret a simple map.**

_____ **Ask for and give the location of places on a map.**
How do you go from _____ to _____?

_____ **Identify places in a community and use direction words to ask for, give, and follow directions on a map.**

school	church	market	movie theater
park	post office	bus stop	bank
right	left	beside	across
corner	go straight	go right	go left

_____ **Apologize for being late and respond to an apology.**
Sorry I'm late.   *Oh, that's okay.*

_____ **Identify other household items.**

pots and pans	tea kettle	broom	glasses
dryer	toaster	dishes	iron
vacuum	trash can	coffee pot	washer
appliances	rocking chair	lamp	ironing board

_____ **Ask for and give prices, and read price labels.**

_____ **Use words of leave-taking.**
So long.   See you tomorrow.

UNIT 7

This is an emergency!

📼 **Listen and read.**

It's starting to rain. José and Van Ly leave the yard sale and walk to the bus stop.

A man is crossing the street. It's Carlos, José's friend. A car is going very fast and hits Carlos. José runs to call 911 and report the traffic accident. He says, "This is an emergency!"

📼 ✏️ **Listen and underline these words in the story.**

1. emergency
2. rain
3. leave
4. crossing
5. street
6. fast
7. hits
8. runs
9. call
10. 911
11. report
12. traffic accident

Read and talk about the underlined words.

Who? What?

Talk about the picture. Use *Who?* and *What?*

✎ **Listen and answer the questions.**

1. Who is leaving the yard sale? _____
2. Who is crossing the street? _____
3. What happens to the man crossing the street? _____
4. What number does José call? _____
5. What does José report? _____
6. What is Van Ly carrying? _____
7. Who is watching the accident? _____
8. What is behind Van Ly? _____

Call 911!

Listen and read.

911.

What's the emergency?

Give me the location with the nearest cross streets.

An emergency team is on the way. Please stay on the phone.

This is an emergency!

There's a traffic accident, and a man is hurt.

It's at the corner of Main Street and Grand Avenue. Please hurry.

Listen and answer.

1. Who is José calling?_____

2. What does he say first?_____

3. What do you think "location" means? _____

4. What are the cross streets? _____

Draw a map of the area around your home with the cross streets.

What's the emergency?

 Listen and read the words.

1. drowning

2. bleeding

3. choking

4. traffic accident

5. robbery

6. fire

 ✏ **Listen and match the words with the pictures.**

1.

4.

_____ a.   choking

_____ b.   fire

___*l*___ c.   drowning

_____ d.   traffic accident

2.

_____ e.   robbery

_____ f.   bleeding

5.

3.

6.

Ask your partner.

911.

What's the emergency?

Give me the location with the nearest cross streets.

An emergency team is on the way. Please stay on the phone.

This is an emergency!

There's _a traffic accident_!

The corner of Main Street and Grand Avenue. Please hurry!

Practice.

1.

a traffic accident

corner of Main and Grand Avenue.

2.

a fire

1414 Oak Street, between Second and Third Avenue.

3.

someone drowning

Centennial Park, between First and Second Avenue.

4.

a robbery

on Main near Orange Avenue.

5.

someone bleeding

4210 Oak Street, Apartment 12 between First and Second Avenue.

6.

someone choking

1894 First Avenue near Main Street.

How's the weather today?

How's the weather today?

It's raining.

Listen and read.

1. raining

2. snowing

3. sunny

4. cloudy

5. windy

6. foggy

7. hot

8. cold

Write about the weather where you live.

Today, in _____ , _____ , it's _____ .
            city   state

It's _____ in _____ , _____ , today.
                      city   state

Ask your partner.

How's the weather today?

It's _____.

Practice.

1. Ask your partner.

   How's the weather today?   It's _____.

2. Point to the pictures and ask *Yes/No* questions.

   Is it raining?   Yes, it is.   (No, it isn't.)

1.

3.

5.

7.

2.

4.

6.

8.

Carlos goes to the Emergency Room.

Listen and read.

The paramedics help Carlos. They take him in the ambulance to the hospital. The doctor and nurse meet Carlos at the door of the emergency room. They examine him carefully.

Carlos fills out the medical form. Now, Carlos is a patient at the hospital.

Listen and answer the questions.

1. Who helps Carlos? _____

2. What takes him to the hospital? _____

3. Who meets Carlos at the hospital? _____

4. What does Carlos fill out? _____

In the Emergency Room.

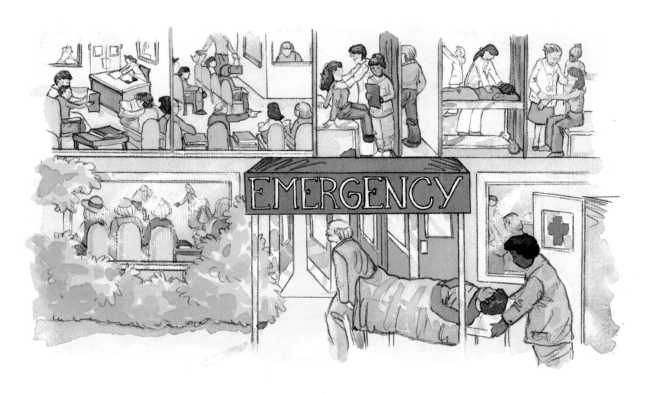

 Listen and read.

1. hospital

2. medical form

3. nurse

4. doctor

5. patient

6. paramedics

7. ambulance

8. emergency room

What's the matter with Carlos?

What's the matter with Carlos? Is his leg hurt?

We don't know yet. We'll look at it.

Listen and read.

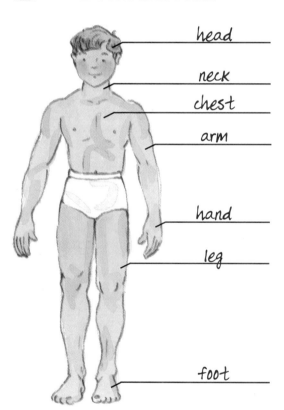

head

neck

chest

arm

hand

leg

foot

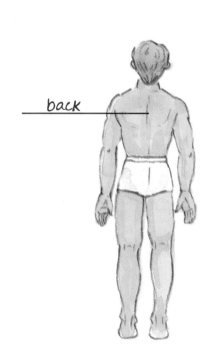

back

Practice. Ask your partner.

What's the matter with Carlos? Is his _____ hurt?

We don't know. We'll look at it.

Review.

✏️ **Match the picture to the words.**

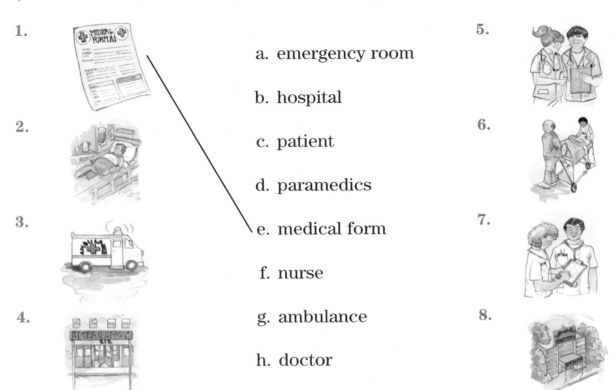

1.

2.

3.

4.

a. emergency room

b. hospital

c. patient

d. paramedics

e. medical form

f. nurse

g. ambulance

h. doctor

5.

6.

7.

8.

Fill in the blanks with these words.

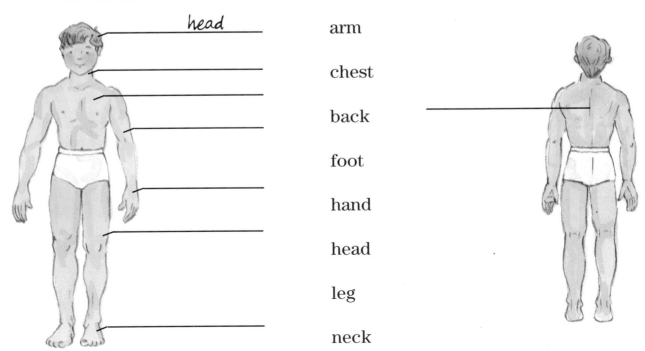

head

arm

chest

back

foot

hand

head

leg

neck

I can do this!

_____ Use a phone to report an emergency—state the kind of emergency and location.

This is an emergency!	Please hurry!
There's a fire.	Someone is drowning.
There's a traffic accident.	There's a robbery.
Someone is choking.	Someone is bleeding.

_____ Ask and talk about the weather. How's the weather today?

It's cold.	It's raining.	It's snowing.	It's sunny.
It's cloudy.	It's windy.	It's foggy.	It's hot.

_____ Identify parts of the body.

head	chest	arm	leg
back	foot/feet	neck	hand

_____ Ask about and discuss injuries.

_____ Use basic emergency, hospital, and medical language.

hospital	medical form	nurse	doctor
patient	paramedic	emergency room	ambulance

Somebody is sick with a cold.

Listen and read.

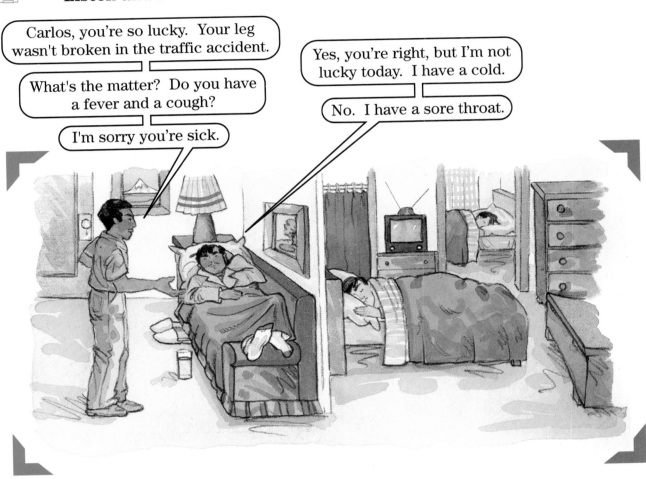

Carlos, you're so lucky. Your leg wasn't broken in the traffic accident.

What's the matter? Do you have a fever and a cough?

I'm sorry you're sick.

Yes, you're right, but I'm not lucky today. I have a cold.

No. I have a sore throat.

Answer the questions.

1. Was Carlos' leg broken in the traffic accident? _____.

2. Who has a cold? _____

3. What's the matter with Carlos? Does he have a fever and a cough?

   _____

4. Does José have a sore throat? _____

5. How are you feeling today? _____

What's the matter?

  Listen and write.

sick

1. Carlos is <u>s i c k</u>.

cold

2. Carmen has a _ _ _ _.

fever

3. Ali has a _ _ _ _ _.

cough

4. Hiroshi has a _ _ _ _ _.

sore throat

5. Petra has a _ _ _ _   _ _ _ _ _ _.

What hurts?

 Listen and write.

back

1. Van's <u>b a c k</u> hurts.

head

2. Rose's _ _ _ _ hurts.

stomach

3. Charlie's _ _ _ _ _ _ _ hurts.

knee

4. Bic's _ _ _ _ hurts.

ear

5. Makeba's _ _ _ hurts.

tooth

6. Pedro's _ _ _ _ _ hurts.

Listen.

  Listen and circle *yes* or *no*.

1. (yes) no

2. yes no

3. yes no

4. yes no

5. yes no

6. yes no

7. yes no

8. yes no

9. yes no

10. yes no

11. yes no

12. yes no

Review.

Listen and read.

How's your father feeling?

What's the matter with him?

That's too bad. What about you? How are you?

That's good.

He's sick.

He has a cold./ His back hurts.

I'm great!

Practice. Use words from the list below.

A. How's your _____ feeling?

B. He's/She's _____.

A. What's the matter with him/her?

B. He/She has a _____. / His/her _____ hurts.

A. That's too bad. What about you? How are you?

B. I'm _____!

A. That's good!/That's too bad.

Family Member		Feeling	Illness	Body Part
father	mother	happy	sore throat	knee
husband	wife	fine	cough	ear
son	daughter	great	fever	tooth
brother	sister	so-so	cold	back
		sad		stomach
		sick		head
		upset		

Ask your partner.

What's the matter with Carlos?

He has a cold.

Ask your partner, listen, and write.

Rose	Petra	Pedro

What's the matter with Rose?

_____

_____

She has a sore throat.

What's the matter with Pedro?

_____

_____

Ali	Hiroshi	Makeba

He has a fever.

What's the matter with Hiroshi?

_____

_____

Her ear hurts.

Ask your partner, listen, and write.

Rose	Ali	Hiroshi
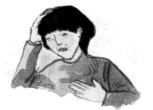		
Her head hurts.	What's the matter with Ali?	He has a cough.
	_____	
	_____	

Pedro	Makeba	Petra

His tooth hurts.	What's the matter with Makeba?	What's the matter with Petra?
	_____	_____
	_____	_____

Feeling better?

José goes to the medicine cabinet to get some medicine for Carlos. He finds some cold medicine and gives some to Carlos.

He makes hot tea

and cooks chicken soup.

Listen and read.

What do you do to feel better when you have a cold?

1.   pills

2.   aspirin

3.   cough syrup

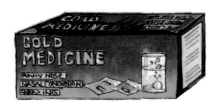

4.   cold medicine

5.   nose drops

6.   ear drops

What's the matter today?

Practice.

What's the matter today?

Sorry to hear that. Do you need some cough syrup?

I have a cough.

Yes, I think I do. Thanks.

What's the matter today?

Sorry to hear that. Do you need some _____?

I have a _____.

Yes, I think I do. Thanks.

1. fever

2. earache

3. toothache

4. sore throat

5. cough

a. pills

b. chicken soup

c. cold medicine

d. hot tea

e. aspirin

f. cough syrup

g. ear drops

h. nose drops

Carlos, Juan, and Pedro share an apartment.

Listen and read.

Carlos, Juan, and Pedro live in an apartment together. Their brothers, sisters, mothers, fathers, wives, sons, and daughters don't live in the U.S.A.

Carlos, Juan, and Pedro stay healthy, work hard, and save their money. They call or write their families every week.

They play football and other games on Saturdays and Sundays.

Listen and write the words.

Carlos, Juan, and Pedro live in an _____ together. Their brothers, sisters,
                                          1

mothers, fathers, wives, _____ and _____ don't live in the U.S.A.
                                2   3

Carlos, Juan, and Pedro stay _____, _____ hard, and _____
                                    4   5   6

their money. They _____ or write their families every week. They
                          7

_____ football and other games on _____ and _____.
     8   9   10

How do Juan, Carlos, and Pedro stay healthy?

 Listen and read.

1. Carlos **showers** every day.

2. Pedro **rests** on Saturdays and Sundays.

3. Juan **brushes** his teeth every day.

4. Juan **sleeps** 8 hours every night.

5. Carlos **eats** fruits and vegetables every day.

6. Pedro **exercises** daily.

What do you do to try to stay healthy? Discuss with your classmates.

Review.

Look back to pages 86 and 94. Make a check on the chart.

		has a fever.	takes a shower every day.	rests on Saturdays and Sundays.	has a cold.	eats fruits and vegetables.	exercises every day.	has a sore throat.	brushes his teeth every day.	has a cough.	lives in an apartment.
1.	Carmen				✔						
2.	Petra										
3.	Ali										
4.	Juan										
5.	Hiroshi										
6.	Pedro										
7.	Carlos										

How do you use it?

Draw a line.

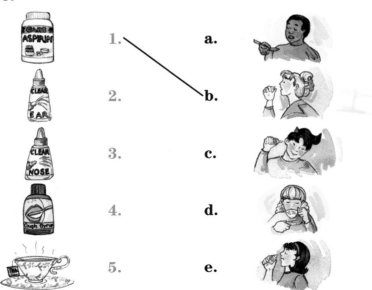

1.   a.

2.   b.

3.   c.

4.   d.

5.   e.

I can do this!

_____ **Use the vocabulary of illness. Ask about and discuss the health of others.**

What's the matter?

How's your mother feeling?

I'm sick.	Carlos is sick.	Ali has a fever.
Hiroshi has a cough.	Petra has a sore throat.	Carmen has a cold.
Van's back hurts.	Makeba's ear hurts.	Bic's knee hurts.
Charlie's stomach hurts.	Pedro's tooth hurts.	Rose's head hurts.

_____ **Identify common medicines and remedies.**

pills	cough syrup	aspirin	cold medicine
ear drops	nose drops	hot tea	chicken soup

_____ **Identify and discuss some good health practices.**

_____ **Use appropriate response to illnesses of others.**

I'm sorry you're sick.   Sorry to hear that.

I	have	a cold.	He	has	a cough.
We		a fever.	She		
They		a sore throat.			

Grandpa wants to take the bus.

Listen and read.

Bye, May. Have fun at school.

Sure, Grandpa. Let's go buy you a bus pass.

Can I take the city bus to my school?

Rose and Van Ly walked May to the bus stop. Now May is getting on the bus.

Rose: Bye, May. Have fun at school!

Van Ly: Can I take the city bus to my school?

Rose: Sure, Grandpa. Let's go buy you a bus pass.

Listen and circle.

D T A
DUTTONVILLE TRANSIT AUTHORITY
Good for one month from date of purchase
Pass for one person
Bus only
3 - 1 - ____   to   3 - 31 - ____

Read the signs on the way to school.

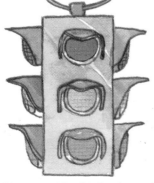

1. The traffic light is red, yellow, and green.

2. Don't park here.

3. Stop your car.

4. Stop! School children are crossing.

5. Don't turn left.

6. Don't go there!

7. Don't turn right.

8. Go out here.

9. Walk now.

Find the signs.

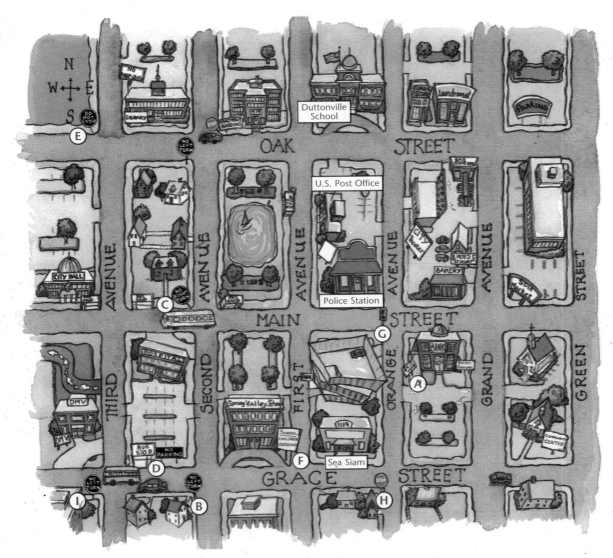

✏️ 💬 **Look at the map and write the letter of the sign.**
Work with a partner.

G 1. Find the **traffic light** at the corner of Orange Avenue and Main Street.

____ 2. Find the **No Parking** sign next to the bus stop.

____ 3. Find the **No Left Turn** sign at the corner of Grace Street and Third Avenue.

____ 4. Find the **Exit** sign at the bank.

____ 5. Find the **Stop** sign at the corner of Grace Street and Orange Avenue.

____ 6. Find the **No Right Turn** sign at the corner of Main Street and Second Avenue.

____ 7. Find the **Do Not Enter** sign on Oak Street.

How do you come to school?

 Listen and read.

    Dominique: How do you come to school?
        Van: I come by bus.
    Carlos: I come by bicycle.

1. by bicycle

2. by motorcycle

3. by car

4. by train

5. on foot

6. by bus

7. by taxi

8. by subway

Practice. Ask your classmate, "How do you come to school?"

Ask your classmates.

Ask your classmates, "How do you come to school?"

	bicycle	subway	motor-cycle	car	train	on foot	bus
1. Van							X
2. Carlos							
3.							
4.							
5.							
6.							
7.							
8.							
9.							
10.							

Complete the bar graph using the information above.

	1	2	3	4	5	6	7	8	9	10	11	12	13	14	15	16	17	18	19	20
by bicycle number ____																				
by subway number ____																				
by motorcycle number ____																				
by car number ____																				
by train number ____																				
on foot number ____																				
by bus number ____																				

Grandpa's ride home on the bus.

🔊 **Listen and read.**

When Grandpa rides the bus home from school, he sees many kinds of stores and places. First, he sees the drugstore. It is next to the laundromat. The movie theater is behind the gas station and the restaurant. The bakery is near the corner of Main Street and Grand Avenue.

🔊 ✏️ **Listen and write the words.**

1. _____drugstore_____

2. _____

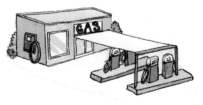

3. _____

4. _____

5. _____

6. _____

Ask your partner.

** Ask your partner.

Listen and write.

Listen to your partner's question.

+ Give the answer.

** 1. I want a dress.
Where should I go?

Go to the department store.

+ a. Go to the gas station.

** 2. I want a cake.
Where should I go?

_____

+ b. Go to the movie theater.

** 3. I want a book.
Where should I go?

_____

+ c. Call 911. Ask for the police.

** 4. I need pills for my headache.
Where should I go?

_____

+ d. Go to the laundromat.

** 5. I want to eat dinner.
Where should I go?

_____

+ e. Go to the post office.

** 6. There is a fire.
Who should I call?

_____

+ f. Go to the Department of Motor
Vehicles (DMV).

Ask your partner.

Student B

Listen to your partner's question.

** Ask your partner.

+ Give the answer.

Listen and write.

+ **1.** Go to the department store.

** a. I need to buy gas.
Where should I go?

_____

+ **2.** Go to the bakery.

** b. I want to see a movie.
Where should I go?

_____

+ **3.** Go to the library.

** c. I need to report a robbery.
Who should I call?

_____

+ **4.** Go to the drug store.

** d. I want to wash my clothes.
Where should I go?

_____

+ **5.** Go to the restaurant.

** e. I need to send a letter.
Where should I go?

_____

+ **6.** Call 911. Ask for the Fire Department.

** f. I need to get my driver's license.
Where should I go?

_____

Can you find the address?

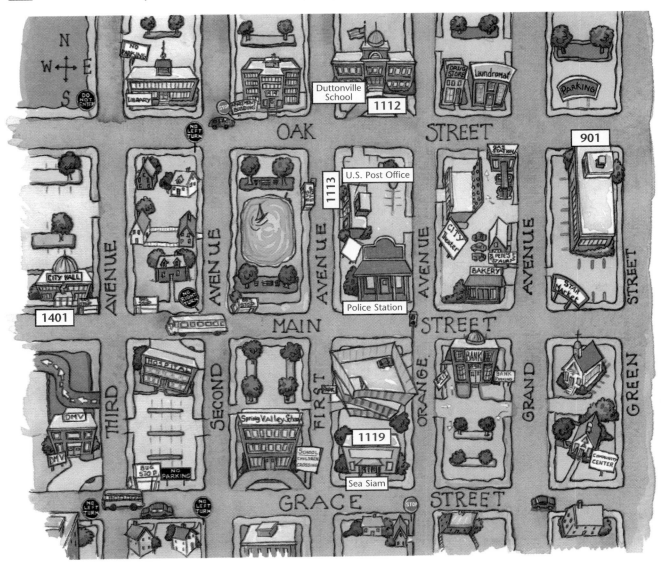

✏ **Read the map and answer the questions.**

1. What can you find at 1119 Grace Street? <u>Sea Siam Restaurant</u>

2. What can you find at 1401 Main Street? _____

3. What is at the NW corner of Main Street and Orange Avenue? _____

4. What is the address of the Duttonville School? _____

5. What is the address of Star Market? _____

6. What is the address of the Post Office? _____

7. Where is Sea Siam Restaurant? It's on _____ Street between _____ Avenue and _____ Avenue. The address is _____.

Can you read a bus schedule?

Duttonville Transit Authority
Bus Schedule # 47 Loop
(East on Oak, south on Grand, west on Grace, north on First)

Oak St. and First Ave. Duttonville School	Oak St. and Orange Ave.	Oak St. and Grand Ave.	Grand Ave. and Main St.	Grand Ave. and Grace St.
8:00 AM	8:10 AM	8:20 AM	8:30 AM	8:40 AM
9:00 AM	9:10 AM	9:20 AM	9:30 AM	9:40 AM
10:00 AM	10:10 AM	10:20 AM	10:30 AM	10:40 AM
11:00 AM	11:10 AM	11:20 AM	11:30 AM	11:40 AM
12:00 PM	12:10 PM	12:20 PM	12:30 PM	12:40 PM
2:00 PM	2:10 PM	2:20 PM		
4:00 PM	4:10 PM		4:30 PM	4:40 PM
6:00 PM	6:10 PM	6:20 PM		6:40 PM
8:00 PM	8:10 PM		8:30 PM	
10:00 PM	10:10 PM	10:20 PM		

Listen and answer.

1. The first bus leaves from Oak and Grand Ave. at __ : __.

2. The last bus leaves Oak and First St. (Duttonville School) at __ : __.

3. How often does Bus #47 leave the Duttonville School every morning? _____

4. How often does Bus #47 leave the Duttonville School every afternoon? _____

5. Fill in the missing times on the bus schedule.

What time does your bus leave?

Duttonville Transit Authority Bus Schedules
Bus #10 (West on Main Street)

Main and Green St.	Main and Orange Ave.	Main and 2nd Ave.	Main and 3rd Ave.
8:00 AM	8:15 AM	8:30 AM	8:45 AM
10:00 AM	10:15 AM	10:30 AM	10:45 AM
11:00 AM	11:15 AM	11:30 AM	11:45 AM
12:00 PM	12:15 PM	12:30 PM	12:45 PM
3:00 PM	3:15 PM	3:30 PM	3:45 PM
6:00 PM	6:15 PM	6:30 PM	6:45 PM

Duttonville Transit Authority Bus Schedule
Bus #47 Loop
(East on Oak, South on Grand, West on Grace, North on First)

Oak St. and First Ave.	Oak St. and Orange Ave.	Oak St. and Grand Ave.	Grand Ave. and Main	Grand Ave. and Grace
8:00 AM	8:10	8:20	8:30	8:40
9:00 AM	9:10	9:20	9:30	9:40
10:00 AM	10:10	10:20	10:30	10:40
11:00 AM	11:10	11:20	11:30	11:40
12:00 PM	12:10	12:20	12:30	12:40
2:00 PM	2:10	2:20	2:30	2:40
4:00 PM	4:10	4:20	4:30	4:40
6:00 PM	6:10	6:20	6:30	6:40
8:00 PM	8:10	8:20	8:30	8:40
10:00 PM	10:10	10:20	10:30	10:40

✎ **Read the schedules and answer the questions.**

1. Grandpa takes Bus # 47 at Oak and First at 2:00 PM.

   He arrives at the Mid-Town Bank at Main and Grand at ___ : ___.

2. Grandpa leaves the bank at 2:45 and catches Bus #10 at Orange Ave. to go home to Main and Second. What bus does he catch? ___ : ___ What times does he get home? ___ : ___

3. Carlos goes to work at Sea Siam Restaurant on Grace Street at 5:00 PM.

   What times does he have to catch Bus 47 at the Duttonville School? ___ : ___

4. Farima is at the Police Station on Main and Orange. It's 3:00 PM.

   Which bus does she take to City Hall at Main and Third? Bus # ____. What time? ___ : ___

5. You are at Duttonville School and have an appointment at the bank at 4:45 PM.

   Which bus do you need to take? Bus # ____. What time? ___ : ___

I can do this.

_____ **Identify and understand basic traffic signals and signs.**

traffic light/signal	No Parking	Stop
School Crossing	No Left Turn	Do Not Enter
No Right Turn	Exit	Walk

_____ **Ask for and give information about transportation.**

_____ **Identify businesses and public places.**

police station	fire department	city hall	library
post office	Department of Motor Vehicles	restaurant	department store
bakery	gas station	movie theater	laundromat

_____ **Read a map.**

_____ **Read and understand a bus schedule.**

_____ **Ask about departure and arrival times of buses.**

_____ **Ask for permission.**
Can I take the bus to school?

_____ **Ask advice.**
Where should I go?   _Who should I call?_

_____ **Express desire and need.**
I want . . .   _I need . . ._

_____ **Make a suggestion.**
Let's go buy . . .

Let's go have coffee.

Listen and read.

Petra:	Let's go have coffee.
Dominique:	Sorry. I have to go to work.
Petra:	Now?
Dominique:	Yes, now. I have two jobs.
Petra:	Two jobs? What do you do?
Dominique:	Well, one is at the bank. It's a full-time job. The other one is at an office.
Petra:	Is that part time?
Dominique:	Yes, it's part time, on weekends only.
Petra:	Well, let's get together some other time.
Dominique:	Okay.

Read and answer the questions.

1. Who wants to have coffee? _____

2. Who has two jobs? _____

3. Where are the two jobs? _____

_____

4. Which job is full time? _____

5. Which job is part time? _____

What job do you want?

Read with your teacher.

Cook Needed. Sea Siam Restaurant  Call 555-2402. Part time $8.00/hr. Sat. and Sun.	**Cobra Inc.**  Factory worker Full time. Call: 555-5111	**Spring Valley Library**  Custodian needed. Part time $4.75/hr. 3 evenings (M-W-F) 555-8360	**City Hall**  Secretary Full time. 555-5600
Tip Top Nails  Wanted! Manicurist Full time. $5.25/hr. 8:00 AM to 6:00 PM (M-F) call: 555-4964	**Duttonville Bank**  Bank Teller Part time. 555-6656	**Nurse Needed!**  Royal Hospital 189 Orange Ave. Full time. Apply in person.	**Joe's Garage**  Part-time Mechanic wanted. Call: 555-7040.

Write the answers.

1. Sea Siam Restaurant needs a _____.

2. Joe's Garage wants a _____.

3. Royal Hospital needs a _____.

4. Tip Top Nails wants a _____.

5. How many full-time jobs are there? _____.

6. What job would you like? _____.

Jobs, jobs, jobs.

Listen, read, and write.

factory worker	teacher	gardener	food server
security guard	nurse	custodian	construction worker
secretary	manicurist	computer entry person	barber

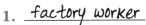   

1. *factory worker*   2. _____   3. _____   4. _____

5. _____   6. _____   7. _____   8. _____

9. _____   10. _____   11. _____   12. _____

What do you do?

What do you do?

I'm a security guard.

Practice with your partner. "I'm a _____ ."

1. I'm a _____ .

Makeba

2. I'm a _____ .

Dominique

3. I'm a _____ .

Hiroshi

4. I'm a _____ .

Carlos

5. I'm a _____ .

Rose

6. I'm a _____ .

Sue

7. I'm a _____ .

Dominique

8. I'm a _____ .

Pedro

9. I'm a _____ .

Juan

Hire or fire.

1. on time

2. late

3. overtime

4. vacation

5. absent

6. hire

7. fire

8. lay off

113

She's on vacation.

on time   absent   hire   vacation

fire   late   lay off   overtime

Listen and circle the correct answer.

1. She's happy. She's _____.
   a. on vacation   b. working overtime

2. Pedro has a new job. The company _____ him today.
   a. hired   b. fired

3. Makeba's car is old and doesn't always work. She is often _____.
   a. on time   b. late

4. Ali is a good worker. He is always _____.
   a. late   b. on time

5. Petra has a cold. She is _____ today.
   a. on vacation   b. absent

6. She is not a good worker.
   The boss _____ her today.
   a. fired   b. hired

7. The company has no work for Hector. The company has _____.
   a. a lay-off   b. overtime

8. The supervisor is asking Rose to work until 7:30 PM.
   She is working _____.
   a. on time   b. overtime.

What do they do?

More Jobs

barber	cook	gardener
house painter	mechanic	bank teller
seamstress	secretary	truck driver

Read and write the job.

1. Ali fixes cars.
He is a _mechanic_.

2. Pedro cuts grass.
He is a _____.

3. Rose types and answers the phone.
She is a _____.

4. Hiroshi cooks.
He is a _____.

5. Karim drives a truck.
He is a _____.

6. Dominique counts money.
She is a _____.

7. Hiroshi's father paints houses.
He is a _____.

8. Petra's mother sews clothes.
She is a _____.

9. Javier cuts hair.
He is a _____.

Interview your classmates.

👥✏️ **Ask your classmates. Write the names of their jobs.**

NAME	JOB

✏️ **Design an ad for the job you want.**

My Dream Job

Name of company: _____

Job: _____

Salary: _____

Hours: _____

Days: _____

Ask your partner.

 Ask your partner and write the answer.
Answer your partner.

1.

What does Ali do?
___Ali fixes cars___.

What is his job?
___He is a mechanic___.

2.

Pedro cuts grass.
He is a gardener.

3.

What does Rose do?
_____.

What is her job?
_____.

4.

Carlos builds houses.
He is a construction worker.

5.

What does Karim do?
_____.

What is his job?
_____.

6.

Farima's sister helps sick people.
She is a nurse.

7.

What does Hiroshi's father do?
_____.

What is his job?
_____.

8.

Petra's mother sews clothes.
She is a seamstress.

9.

What does Javier do?
_____.

What is his job?
_____.

Ask your partner

Student B

🗣🗣 ✏ **Ask your partner and write the answer.**
Answer your partner.

1. Ali fixes cars. He is a mechanic.	2.  What does Pedro do? _____. What is his job? _____.	3. Rose types and answers the phone. She is a secretary.
4.  What does Carlos do? _____. What is his job? _____.	5.  Karim drives a truck. He is a truck driver.	6.  What does Farima's sister do? _____. What is her job? _____.
7.  Hiroshi's father paints houses. He is a house painter.	8.  What does Petra's mother do? _____. What is her job? _____.	9.  Javier cuts hair. He is a barber.

Carmen applies for a job.

Read Carmen's application with your teacher.

Employment Application

Name __Castro__ __Carmen__ __Luz__
        (last)   (first)   (middle name)

Address __3496 N. Third St.__ Apt # __6B__

City __Clarkton__ State __CA__ Zip Code __92204__

Telephone __501__ __555-7286__ Social Security Number __109__ __56__ __6228__

When can you start? __Now__

Are you available to work ☑ Full Time? ☐ Part Time?

Check shift you can work.

☑ 7 AM–3 PM (First) ☐ 3 PM–11 PM (Second) ☐ 11 PM–7 AM (Third)

Fill out your own job application.

Employment Application

Name _____
        (last)   (first)   (middle name)

Address _____ Apt # _____

City _____ State _____ Zip Code _____

Telephone ____ _____ Social Security Number ____ ____ ____

When can you start? _____

Are you available to work ☐ Full Time? ☐ Part Time?

Check shift you can work.

☐ 7 AM–3 PM (First) ☐ 3 PM–11 PM (Second) ☐ 11 PM–7 AM (Third)

I can do this.

_____ **Identify occupations and occupational activities.**

barber	bank teller	cook	
construction worker	custodian	factory worker	food server
gardener	house painter	manicurist	mechanic
nurse	seamstress	secretary	security guard
computer entry person	teacher	truck driver	

_____ **Identify employment vocabulary.**

on time	late	absent	hire
overtime	vacation	full time	part time
fire	lay off		

_____ **Read basic job ads.**

_____ **Fill out an employment application.**

_____ **Make a suggestion/Offer an invitation.**
Let's go have coffee.

_____ **Express regret or decline an invitation and state a reason.**
Sorry, I have to work.

_____ **Express necessity.**   _I have to work._

UNIT 11

Dad works so hard.

Listen and read.

The Duval family is eating dinner. They are talking.

Jack: I'm tired. I'm working so hard.
Dominique: Me, too. I go to school at night and work every day.
Grandpa: Jack, can we help you at your office?
Jack: Thanks. Can you come on Saturday?

Read and answer the questions.

1. What is the Duval family doing? _____

2. Who goes to school at night and works every day? _____

3. Who is tired? _____

4. Where are they going on Saturday? _____

5. What do you think they're eating for dinner? _____

Jack's office.

Listen and read.

1. file cabinet
2. adding machine
3. copier
4. fax machine
5. calculator

6. telephone answering machine
7. computer screen
8. computer keyboard
9. wastebasket
10. typewriter

At the office.

1. adding machine
2. calculator
3. calendar
4. chair
5. clock
6. computer keyboard
7. table

8. copier
9. desk
10. fax machine
11. file cabinet
12. notebook
13. pencil
14. pencil sharpener

15. typewriter
16. wastebasket
17. computer screen
18. telephone answering machine

Practice.

1. Point and ask your partner: Is this a _____? Yes, it is. (No, it isn't.)

2. Point and ask your partner: What is this? It's a _____.

3. Ask your partner to point: Where is the _____? Here it is.

Review.

Listen, read, and write the letter.

__H__   1.   The file cabinet is next to the door.

_____   2.   One wastebasket is between the fax machine and the typewriter.

_____   3.   The adding machine is to the right of the computer.

_____   4.   The telephone answering machine is on the table.

_____   5.   The computer is to the right of the calendar.

_____   6.   The fax machine is to the left of the computer.

_____   7.   The other wastebasket is under the table.

_____   8.   The calculator is beside the answering machine.

Review.

Fill in your own information.

Today's Date _____
                    month   date   year

Name: _____
            last   first   middle

Home Address: _____
                  number and street   (apartment)

_____
        city   state   zip code

Home phone: _____ _____   Work phone: _____ _____

Date of birth: _____
              month—date—year

Listen. Find the letters you hear.

Don't touch! The machine is hot!

Listen and read.

Let's be safe!

Listen and read.

a. Women

b. Men

c. Quiet!

d. Keep Out

e. EXIT

f. Phone

g. Emergency Exit Only

h. CAUTION

i. DO NOT TOUCH!

j. DANGER

k. DO NOT ENTER

l. NO SMOKING

Read, and write the letter of the sign.

L _ 1. You can't smoke here.

____ 2. No! Stay out!

____ 3. This way to the telephone.

____ 4. Don't go in there.

____ 5. Sh-h-h-h-h!

____ 6. Men's restroom.

____ 7. In an emergency, go this way.

____ 8. Go out here every day.

____ 9. Be careful! Be cautious!

____ 10. Women's restroom.

____ 11. Big trouble! Very dangerous.

____ 12. Do not come near.

They're helping Dad at work.

Listen and read.

1. Jack is sending a fax.

2. Dominique is using the computer.

3. Thérèse is typing a letter.

4. Gigi is using the calculator.

5. George is talking on the telephone.

6. Grandpa Duval is filing papers.

7. Dominique is making copies.

8. Grandpa Duval is emptying the waste basket.

9. Jack is using the clothes-pressing machine.

Ask your partner.   Student A

** Ask your partner and write the answer.

1. **What is **George** doing?
   George is talking on the phone.

3. **What is **Petra's mother** doing?
   _____

5. ** What is **Therese** doing?
   _____

7. **What **Gigi** doing?
   _____

9. **What is **Javier** doing?
   _____

11. **What is **Farima's sister** doing?
    _____

+ Answer your partner.

+ **Jack** is sending a fax.

+ **Dominique** is using the computer.

+ **Hiroshi's father** is painting a house.

+ **Karim** is driving a truck.

+ **Grandpa Duval** is filing papers.

+ **Pedro** is fixing the car.

Ask your partner. Student B

2. **What is **Karim** doing?

_____

4. **What is **Jack** doing?

_____

6. ** What is **Dominique** doing?

_____

8. **What is **Pedro** doing?

_____

10. **What is **Grandpa Duval** doing?

_____

12. **What is **Hiroshi's father** doing?

_____

+ Answer your partner.

+ **Javier** is cutting hair.

+ **Therese** is typing a letter.

+ **Petra's mother** is sewing clothes.

+ **George** is talking on the phone.

+ **Farima's sister** is helping sick people.

+ **Gigi** is using a calculator.

Review.

verb + s		
cleans	builds	sews
cuts	helps	cooks
drives	paints	types

What does she do at her job? What does he do at his job? Write the correct answer.

1. Hiroshi is a cook. He _____*COOKS*_____ at the restaurant.

2. Carlos is a construction worker. He _____ houses.

3. Karim is a truck driver. He _____ a truck.

4. Farima's sister is a nurse. She _____ sick people.

5. Javier is a barber. He _____ hair.

Write the number of the correct picture on the line.

_____ Juan is a security guard.

_____ Makeba is a manicurist.

_____ Carlos is a construction worker.

_____ Rose is a secretary.

_____ Carmen is a seamstress in a factory.

I can do this.

_____ **Ask for and give information about work.**

_____ **Use vocabulary of jobs and employment.**

_____ **Identify basic office equipment and furniture.**

file cabinet	computer keyboard	telephone answering machine
fax machine	adding machine	computer screen/monitor
copier	calculator	wastebasket
typewriter		

_____ **Read, identify, and understand basic public signs.**

Quiet	Keep out	Exit	Telephone
Men	Emergency Exit	Caution	Do Not Touch
Women	No Smoking	Danger	Do Not Enter

_____ **Express warning or caution.**
Be careful!   Don't touch!

_____ **Offer help.**
Jack, can we help you at your office?   Let me help you.

_____ **Make a request.**
Can you come on Saturday?

_____ **Make commands.**
Please, read the signs. Don't have an accident.

_____ **Use verb + _ing_ and verb + _s_ structures appropriately.**

verb + _ing_		verb	
I'm		I	type every day.
He's		You	
She's	working now.	We	file papers.
We're		They	make copies.
They're		**verb + _s_**	
You're		He	types every day.
		She	fixes the car.
			teaches.

What's the problem?

🔲 **Listen and read.**

Carlos, Juan, and Pedro have many problems in their apartment. Look at the picture. Talk with your teacher. Draw a circle around each problem. How many problems can you find?

I found _____ problems in the apartment.

Do you have problems in your house or apartment? What kind of problems?

The roof is leaking.

Listen and read.

1. The roof is leaking.

2. The window is cracked.

3. The faucet is dripping.

4. The toilet is overflowing.

5. The stove is broken.

6. The television isn't working.

7. The heat isn't working.

8. The shower isn't working.

9. The refrigerator is leaking.

The window is cracked.

✎ **Read and write.**

a. The window is cracked.
b. The toilet is overflowing.
c. The stove is broken.

d. The roof is leaking.
e. The faucet is dripping.
f. The refrigerator is leaking.

g. The heat isn't working.
h. The shower isn't working.
i. The television isn't working.

1. _The roof is leaking._

2. _____

3. _____

4. _____

5. _____

6. _____

7. _____

8. _____

9. _____

Yes, I'm the manager.

Listen and read.

Hello. This is Carlos in apartment 19 K. Is this the manager?

We have a problem in our apartment.

The roof is leaking. Can you come over?

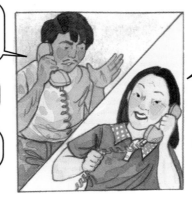

Yes, I'm the manager.

I'm sorry. What's the problem?

Sure, I'll be right over.

Practice.

You

Hello, this is _____ in _____. Is this the manager?

We have a problem in our _____.

The _____. Can you come over?

Your partner

Yes, I'm the manager.

I'm sorry. What's the problem?

Sure, I'll be right over.

1.

2.

3.

4.

5.

6.

7.

8.

Who fixes the problems?

 Listen and read.

1. The **plumber** fixes the faucet, the shower, and the toilet.

2. The **repairperson** fixes the roof and the window.

3. The **electrician** fixes the refrigerator, the stove, and the heat.

4. The **TV repairperson** fixes the VCR and the television.

Write your own note.

_____, _____
month - date   year

Dear Manager,

    I live in apartment __B__,
and the ___toilet___ is ___overflowing___.

Would you please call the ___plumber___
to repair it as soon as possible?

    Thank you.

    Sincerely,
___Hiroshi Tanaka___

_____, _____
month - date   year

Dear Manager,

_____

_____

_____

_____

    Sincerely,

_____

The stove is broken.

What's the problem?

Oh! I'll call the electrician.

My stove is broken.

You

What's the problem?

Oh! I'll call the _____.

Your Partner

My _____.

Practice.

1.

2.

3.

4.

5.

6.

7.

8.

9.

We need to move.

Listen and read.

José: Carlos, you need to move.

Carlos: Yes, José. You're right!

José: This apartment has too many problems.

Carlos: Let's look for a house together.

José: Okay. Let's look in the paper.

✏️ **Read and answer the questions.**

1. Why does Carlos want to move? _____

2. Where do Carlos and José want to move? _____

3. Why are they going to look in a newspaper? _____

4. What are the problems in the apartment?

_____

_____

_____

_____

_____

_____

The Spring Valley News.

Read and discuss with your teacher.

Classified Ads.

1. HOUSE FOR RENT
$950/month
2 bedrooms
1 bathroom
Near school.
Call (715) 555-1434

2. HOUSE—321 Park Ave.
$1025/month
3 bedrooms
2 bathrooms
Furnished—washer, dryer, stove, and refrigerator.
OPEN HOUSE   9–5 daily
555-8735

3. Clean Apartment
$725/month
3 bedrooms
2 baths
No pets.
Near shopping.
Call 555-3460

4. House for Sale
NEW! CLEAN!
Near park/school.
3 bedrooms with 2 baths
$150,000
Call (714) 555-4170

5. FOR RENT
3 BDR. HOUSE/2 BATHS
Unfurnished.
Near bus stop.
Near shopping mall.
Call JONES REALTY
555-9430

6. NEW HOUSE FOR RENT
3 bedrooms
2 bathrooms
Large yard.
Furnished.
Near library and school.
Open House: 8–5 daily
555-9321

7. Small Apartment
Quiet
1 bedroom—1 bath
$325
(714) 555-1004

✎ **Read and answer the questions.**

Look at 1.   How many bedrooms does the house have? _____

Look at 2.   Is it for rent? Yes / No

Look at 3.   Is this an apartment or a house? _____

Look at 4.   Is it for sale? Yes / No

Look at 5.   Can you call for information? Yes / No

Look at 6.   Is it furnished? Yes / No

Look at 7.   What is the rent? _____

Talk about it.

Spring Valley News Classified Ads

1. HOUSE FOR RENT
$950/month
2 Bedrooms
1 bathroom
Near School.
Call (715) 555-1434

2. HOUSE—321 Park Ave.
$1025/month
3 bedrooms
2 bathrooms
Furnished—washer, dryer,
    stove, and refrigerator.
OPEN HOUSE   9–5 daily
                        555-8735

3. Clean Apartment
$725/month
3 bedrooms
2 baths
No pets.
Near shopping.
Call 555-3460

4. House for Sale
NEW! CLEAN!
Near park/school.
3 bedrooms with 2 baths
$150,000
Call (714) 555-4170

5. FOR RENT
3 BDR. HOUSE/2 BATHS
Unfurnished.
Near bus stop.
Near shopping mall.
Call JONES REALTY
555-9430

6. NEW HOUSE FOR RENT
3 bedrooms
2 bathrooms
Large yard.
Furnished.
Near library and school.
Open House: 8–5 daily
555-9321

7. Small Apartment
Quiet
1 bedroom—1 bath
$325
(714) 555-1004

Practice with your partner using the information above.

Hello.

Yes, it is. May I help you?

Yes. Would you like to see it?

Sure! See you then.

Is this _555-9321_ ?

Yes, I'm calling about the ___house___ for rent.
It has 3 bedrooms and 2 baths.
Is it still available?

Great. Can we come today at 3:00?

New house for rent.

Listen and read.

José and Carlos are with the owner. She is showing the house.

Owner: Let me show you this house.
Carlos: The yard is nice and large.
José: It's a big, beautiful house.
Owner: It's a two-story house, and it's furnished.
Carlos: We're bringing our families to the United States.
José: How much is the rent?

Discuss rents in your area and decide the rent for this house.
Owner: It's _____ a month.

Do you like this house?

Listen and write.

Carlos and José like the house very much. Help them with their questions.

1. How many bedrooms are there downstairs? _____

2. How many bedrooms are there upstairs? _____

3. Is there a stove in the kitchen? _____

4. What room is between the bedroom and the kitchen? _____

5. Is there a sofa in the living room? _____

6. Is there a washer and dryer in the garage? _____

7. Are there two bathrooms downstairs? _____

8. Do you see a shower in the downstairs bathroom? _____

Practice. Interview your classmate.

How many do you have?   Write the number.

_____ sofa	_____ bedroom	_____ shower
_____ table	_____ bathroom	_____ tub
_____ bed	_____ kitchen	_____ door
_____ chair	_____ living room	_____ window
_____ lamp	_____ refrigerator	_____ garage
_____ dresser	_____ washer and dryer	_____ sink

I can do this!

_____ Identify and report household repair needs.

The window is cracked.	The roof is leaking.	The heat isn't working.
The toilet is overflowing.	The faucet is dripping.	The shower isn't working.
The stove is broken.	The refrigerator is leaking.	The television isn't working.

_____ Identify repairpersons.

The plumber fixes the faucet, shower, and toilet.	The repairperson fixes the roof and the window.
The electrician fixes the refrigerator, the stove, and the heat.	The TV repairperson fixes the VCR and the television.

_____ Call the manager, describe the problem, and request household repairs.

_____ Read and compare housing ads.

_____ Call and ask questions about housing ads.

_____ Make an appointment to check on housing.

_____ Write a simple note requesting household repairs.

It's a deal!

Listen and read.

José and Carlos like the house. They want to rent it. The price is right!
"It's a deal!" José and Carlos say. They shake hands with the owner.
Carlos says, " We have a lot to do."
José says, " Yes, we have to go to the bank, to the post office, and to City Hall."

Circle the correct answer.

1. Are José and Carlos buying the house? Yes / No

2. Is the rent too high?   Yes / No

3. "It's a deal!" means   a.   No, I don't want to do this.

   b.   Yes, I want to do this.

4. "Shake hands" means a.   We aren't happy.

   b.   We agree.

Why do they need to go to the bank, to the post office, and to City Hall?

Carlos goes to the bank.

Spring Valley Bank

Hi! I need a money order.

Listen and read.

1. cash

2. credit card

3. ATM machine

4. ATM card

5. check

6. checking account

7. money order

Need some money?

Write. Draw a line and write the word.

1. _____ ATM machine _____

a. credit card

2. _____

b. check

3. _____

c. ATM machine

4. _____

d. checking account

5. _____

e. money order

6. _____

f. cash

7. _____

g. ATM card

I need a money order.

"Hi! I need a money order."

Read and match.

"I need to open a checking account." _e_

a. "Sure. We take credit cards."

"Where's the ATM machine?" ___

b. "How much cash do you need?

"I need some cash." ___

c. "Look in your wallet/purse."

"Can I use my credit card?" ___

d. "Next to that store."

"Where's my ATM card?' ___

e. "Okay. Please let me help you."

"Can I write a check?" ___

f. "Sorry, no checks. We only take cash."

"I need a money order." ___

g. "Okay. I'm happy to help you with your money order."

Can I have a Change of Address form?

Duttonville Post Office

Listen and read.

1. stamps

2. letter

3. package

Change of address for: ☐ Individual ☐ Family
Is this move temporary? ☐ YES ☐ NO
Start date: (month/day/year) ☐ ☐ ☐ ☐ ☐

Print First Name: ☐☐☐☐☐☐☐☐☐☐
Print Last Name: ☐☐☐☐☐☐☐☐☐☐

Print OLD mailing address: ☐☐☐☐
☐☐☐☐☐☐☐☐☐☐☐☐☐☐
Print NEW mailing address:
☐☐☐☐☐☐☐☐☐☐☐☐☐☐
Sign and print name below.
Sign_____
Print_____

4. Change of Address form

CAPE COD, MA

5. post card

Bank of USA — DATE _____ 19 __
MONEY ORDER

PAY TO _____

AMOUNT _____ $ ____

Signature _____ Address _____
003479:16790-0902

6. money order

  Underline the words you hear.

149
• • • •

What do you need at the post office?

Write. Draw a line and write the word.

1. _____ *package* _____

a. **letter**

2. _____

b. **post card**

3. _____

c. **Change of Address form**

| Bank of USA | DATE _____ 19 ___ |
| MONEY ORDER | |
| PAY TO _____ |
| AMOUNT _____ $ _____ |
| Signature _____ Address _____ |
| 003479:16790-0902 | |

4. _____

d. **package**

5. _____

e. **stamps**

Change of address for: ☐ Individual ☐ Family
Is this move temporary? ☐ YES ☐ NO
Start date: (month/day/year) ☐☐ ☐☐ ☐☐

Print First Name: ☐☐☐☐☐☐☐☐☐☐☐
Print Last Name: ☐☐☐☐☐☐☐☐☐☐☐

Print OLD mailing address: ☐☐☐☐☐☐☐☐☐
☐☐☐☐☐☐☐☐☐☐☐
Print NEW mailing address: ☐☐☐☐☐☐☐
☐☐☐☐☐☐☐☐☐☐☐
Sign and print name below.
Sign_____
Print_____

f. **money order**

6. _____

I need to mail a package.

Read and match.

"I need to mail a package." _b_

"I want to buy some stamps." ___

"How much for a post card?" ___

"I need a Change of Address form." ___

"I want to send a letter." ___

"I want to buy a money order." ___

a. "Okay. Do you know the zip code?"

b. "Where is your package going?"

c. "How many stamps do you need?"

d. "Sure. How much money do you want to send?"

e. "Post cards are 20 cents."

f. "When are you moving?"

Practice.

Where can you buy money orders?

✎ **Write. Fill out the money order below.**

Date: _____
               (today's date)

Pay to: _____
           (ask your teacher)

Bank of USA
MONEY ORDER

DATE _____ 19 ____

PAY TO _____

AMOUNT _____ $ _____

Signature _____   Address _____
003479:16790-0902

Review these numbers.

11	eleven	21	twenty-one	70	seventy
12	twelve	22	twenty-two	77	seventy-seven
13	thirteen	30	thirty	80	eighty
14	fourteen	33	thirty-three	88	eighty-eight
15	fifteen	40	forty	90	ninety
16	sixteen	44	forty-four	100	one hundred
17	seventeen	50	fifty	250	two hundred fifty
18	eighteen	55	fifty-five	500	five hundred
19	nineteen	60	sixty	1,000	one thousand
20	twenty	66	sixty-six		

Ask your partner.   *Student A*

** **Give directions and spell the word for your partner.**
+ **Write the answer.**

 **1.** ** Find the check. **Write: c - h - e - c - k	 **2.** + _____
 **3.** + _____	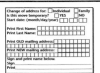 **4.** **Find the ATM card. **Write: A - T - M c - a - r - d
 **5.** **Find the cash. **Write: c - a - s - h	 **6.** + _____
7. + _____	 **8.** **Find the letter. ** Write: l - e - t - t - e - r
 **9.** **Find the ATM machine. **Write A - T - M m - a - c - h - i - n - e	 **10.** + _____
 **11.** + _____	**12.** **Find the package. **Write: p - a - c - k - a - g - e

Ask your partner.   **Student B**

** **Give directions and spell the word for your partner.**
+ **Write the answer.**

 (check) **1.** + _____	 **2.** ** Find the credit card. **Write: c - r - e - d - i - t c - a - r - d
 (money order) **3.** **Find the money order. **Write: m - o - n - e - y o - r - d - e - r	 **4.** + _____
 (money) **5.** + _____	 **6.** **Find the change of address form. **Write: c - h - a - n - g - e o - f a - d - d - r - e - s - s
(stamps) **7.** **Find the stamps. ** Write: s - t - a - m - p - s	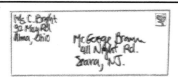 **8.** + _____
 (ATM) **9.** + _____	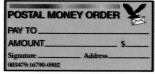 **10.** **Find the money order. **Write : m - o - n - e - y o - r - d - e - r
 (post card) **11.** **Find the post card. **Write: p - o - s - t c - a - r - d	 **12.** + _____

It'll be very cold next month.

It'll be very cold next month.

Yes, it will be. What month are your wife and daughter moving here to Duttonville?

Listen and read.

José and Carlos are going to Duttonville City Hall to pay for their utilities—new phone, lights, and heat.

José: It'll be very cold next month.

Carlos: Yes, it will be. What month are your wife and daughter moving here to Duttonville?

What month do you think they're coming?

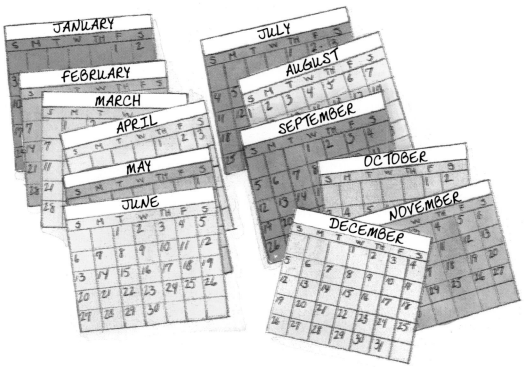

I can do this.

_____ **Identify community institutions and services:**
bank, post office, City Hall

_____ **Understand the concept of a final agreement.**
"It's a deal."   _"Let's shake hands."_

_____ **Identify and access banking services.**

cash	credit card	ATM card	ATM machine
checking account	money order	check	

_____ **Identify and access postal services.**

stamps	letter	package
post card	money order	Change of Address form

_____ **Fill out a money order form.**

_____ **Inquire about services.**

Where's the ATM machine?	Can I use my credit card?
Where's my ATM card?	Can I write a check?
How much for a post card?	

_____ **Request service and state need.**

I need to open a checking account.	I need some cash.
I need a money order.	I want to buy some stamps.
I need to buy a money order.	I need a Change of Address form.
I want to send a letter.	I need to mail a package.

_____ **Talk about and express a future event.**
It'll be very cold next month.

Those kids!

Bic, you're lazy at home. I don't like your clothes. You don't look clean. Your room is messy. You come home late. You drive too fast. Your car is too noisy. You smoke too much.

What about Kim? She talks on the phone all day. She wears too much makeup. Her skirts are too short.

Listen and read.

Rose is upset with her son and daughter. She is angry.

Rose: Bic, you're lazy at home. I don't like your clothes. You don't look clean. Your room is messy. You come home late. You drive too fast. Your car is too noisy. You smoke too much.

Bic: What about Kim? She talks on the phone all day. She wears too much makeup. Her skirts are too short.

Discuss with your classmates.

What do you think about Rose and her son and daughter?

Are you angry? Are you pleased?

Listen and read.

a. angry

b. pleased

c. lazy

d. hard-working

e. dirty

f. clean

g. messy

h. neat

i. late

j. early

k. fast

l. slow

m. noisy

n. quiet

o. too little

p. too much

Underline the words you hear.

Complete the sentences.

1. I am _____.

2. My house is _____.

3. My classroom is _____.

Bic drives too fast.

Circle the word you like.

		a.		b.	
1.	Bic's car is very	a.	fast.	b.	slow.
2.	Rose is	a.	upset.	b.	pleased.
3.	Bic's clothes are	a.	dirty.	b.	clean.
4.	Kim talks on the phone	a.	too little.	b.	too much.
5.	Rose cleans house all day. She is	a.	lazy.	b.	hard-working.
6.	Rose says Bic's room is	a.	neat.	b.	messy.
7.	Bic comes home	a.	early.	b.	late.
8.	Bic's car is very	a.	noisy.	b.	quiet.

Do you come to school early or late?

I come late.

Practice.
What about you?

		a.		b.	
1.	Do you come to school	a.	late?	b.	early?
2.	Are you	a.	noisy?	b.	quiet?
3.	Is your house	a.	messy?	b.	neat?
4.	Are your clothes	a.	clean?	b.	dirty?
5.	Do you have	a. b.	too much homework? too little homework?		
6.	Is your car	a.	too fast?	b.	too slow?
7.	At school, are you	a.	lazy?	b.	hard-working?

Who likes what?

Write the words in the chart.

fast cars	cigarettes	makeup	talking on the phone
short skirts	noisy cars	lazy son	coming home late
messy room	clean clothes	neat room	

Bic

likes	doesn't like
fast cars	makeup

Rose

likes	doesn't like

Kim

likes	doesn't like

Practice. Talk with your partner. Use the above information.

Bic likes _fast cars_.

He doesn't like _neat rooms_.

Rose likes _____.

She doesn't like _____.

Take a message.

Listen and read.

Stacey: Hello, this is Stacey. Can I speak to Kim?

Bic: Sorry, Kim isn't here. This is Bic, her brother. Can I take a message?

Stacey: Yes, please tell her I called. My number is 702-555-9702.

Bic: 703-555-9702 ?

Stacey: No, 702.

Bic: Oh! 702-555-9702.

Stacey: That's right.

Bic: Okay, I'll have her call you.

Stacey: Thanks. Good-bye.

Bic: Bye!

Write the phone message.

Phone Message

For: ___Kim_____

From: _____

Time: _____

_____ Will call back.   _____ Please call.

Phone: _____

Hello, can I speak to...?

You		Your Partner

You

Hello, this is _____.
Can I speak to _____.

Yes, please tell _____ I called. My number is _____.

No, _____.

That's right.

Thanks. Good-bye.

Your Partner

Sorry, _____ isn't here. Can I take a message?

_____?

Oh! _____.

Okay, I'll have _____ call you.

Bye!

 Practice.

Petra
Ali
 	
                   Ali
him
701-555-8274
 	
              703-555-8274?
No! 701-555-8274
 	
              701-555-8274.
              him
	Karim
	Mohammed
	
	              Mohammed
	him
	416-555-3467
	
	              416-555-3467
	No! 416-555-3467
	
	              416-555-3467.
	              him

Makeba
Pedro
 	
              Pedro
him
714-555-1243
 	
              714-555-1324?
No! 714-555-1243
 	
              714-555-1243.
              him
	José
	Van
	
	              Van
	him
	814-555-4949
	
	              814-555-9494?
	No! 814-555-4949
	
	              814-555-4949
	              him

Ask your partner.   *Student A*

** Caller, please leave your message.

+ Please take the message.

1.

> Hello, we're not at home now, and we're sorry to have missed your call. Please leave the date and time you called and a short message. Have a nice day.

**

Hi, Margo. This is Louisa. It's 2:30 on Tuesday, April 5. Please call me at area code (405) 555-1191. Good-bye!

2.

> Hello, I'm sorry to have missed your call. Your call is important to me, so please leave the date and time you called and a short message. Have a good day.

+

For: _____

From: _____

Time: _____ *Date:* _____

Phone: _____

Message: _____

_____

_____

3.

> Hello, we're not at home now, and we're sorry to miss your call. Please leave the date and time you called and a short message. Have a good day.

**

Kay, this is Grace. Sorry to miss you. It's now 4:30 on Wednesday. Please call me when you get in. I can be reached at (714) 555-5111. Talk to you later.

Bye!

4.

> Hello, we're not at home now and are sorry to miss your call. Please leave the date and time you called and a short message. Have a good day.

+

For: _____

From: _____

Time: _____ *Date:* _____

Phone: _____

Message: _____

_____

_____

Ask your partner.

Student B

** Caller, please leave your message.

+ Please take the message.

1.

Hello, we're not at home now, and we're sorry to have missed your call. Please leave the date and time you called and a short message. Have a good day.

+

For: _____

From: _____

Time: _____ *Date:* _____

Phone: _____

Message: _____

_____

_____

2.

Hello, I'm sorry to have missed your call. Your call is important to me, so please leave the date and time you called and a short message. Have a good day.

**

Hello, Mother. This is your son, Ibrahim. It's 4:00 PM on Tuesday. Please call me tonight. Love you. Bye.

3.

Hello, we're not at home now, and we're sorry to miss your call. Please leave the date and time you called and a short message. Have a good day.

+

For: _____

From: _____

Time: _____ *Date:* _____

Phone: _____

Message: _____

_____

_____

4.

Hello, we're not at home now and are sorry to miss your call. Please leave the date and time you called and a short message. Have a good day.

**

Hello, Van Ly, this is your teacher, Ms. Apple. It's now 6:30 on Monday evening. I'm sorry you were absent from school today. We missed you. I hope everything is okay, and I hope to see you tomorrow. If you can't come to school, please call me at 555-8360. Good-bye.

You kids!

> You kids!
> I don't like the way you dress!

Listen and read.

Rose doesn't like the way Bic and Kim dress. She says, "Bic, your shorts are too long, and your shirt is too large. Kim, your blouse is too small, and your skirt is too short." She also thinks that Kim is too thin and that Bic's hair is too curly.

Listen and write the word under the correct picture.

a. short	b. long	c. small	d. large
e. thin	f. heavy	g. curly	h. straight

1. _____

2. _____

3. _____

4. _____

5. _____

6. _____

7. _____

8. _____

Kim likes makeup!

Listen and read.

Kim wants to be beautiful. She likes makeup very much. She makes her lips red. She makes her cheeks pink. She makes her eyebrows and eyelashes black. She brushes her teeth in the morning and at night. They are clean and white. She wears earrings and a necklace. She loves makeup.

a. eyes	b. neck	c. mouth	d. eyelashes	e. eyebrow
f. cheek	g. ear	h. teeth	i. nose	

Listen and write the word under the correct picture.

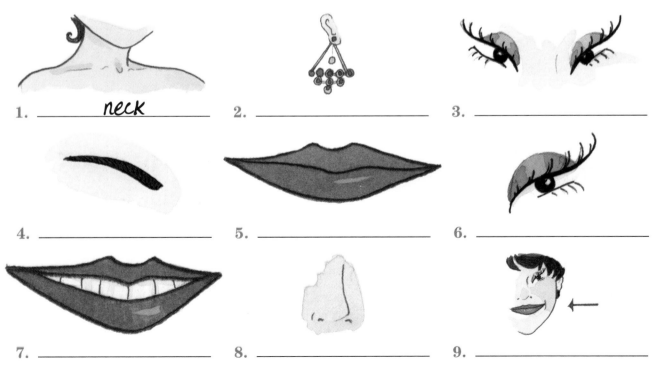

1. _____ *neck* _____

2. _____

3. _____

4. _____

5. _____

6. _____

7. _____

8. _____

9. _____

Review.

This is Kim.

Write the word on the line.

cheek

eyelashes

nose

lips/mouth

eye

eyebrow

teeth

ear

neck

① *eyebrow*

②

④

⑥

⑦

③

⑤

⑧

⑨

Draw a necklace on Kim.
Draw earrings on Kim.

This is Bic.

Write the word.

arm

back

chest

elbow

fingers

foot/feet

hand

head

knee

leg

wrist

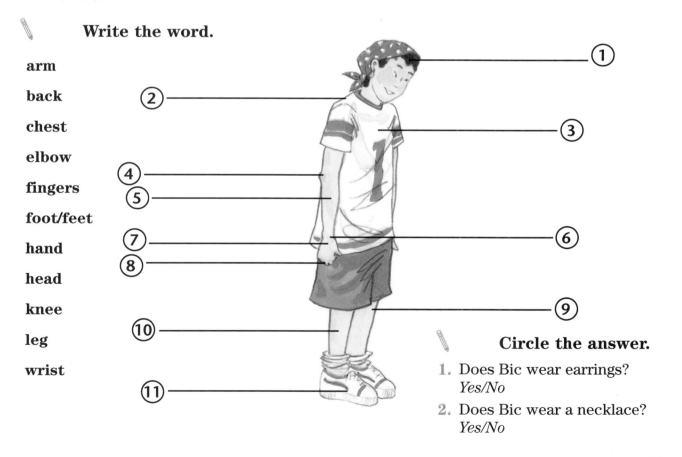

Circle the answer.

1. Does Bic wear earrings?
   Yes/No
2. Does Bic wear a necklace?
   Yes/No

I can do this.

_____ **Expand vocabulary through the use of antonyms.**

angry	pleased	lazy	hard-working
dirty	clean	messy	neat
too much	too little	late	early
fast	slow	noisy	quiet
short	long	small	big
thin	heavy	curly	straight

_____ **Express likes and dislikes.**

_____ **Use telephone vocabulary in giving and receiving telephone messages.**
Can I take a message?   *Tell her I called.*

_____ **Expand and review vocabulary of body parts.**

arm	back	cheek	chest	ear
elbow	eye	eyebrow	eyelash	fingers
foot/feet	hand	head	knee	leg
mouth/lip	neck	nose	teeth	wrist

_____ **Ask for and state opinion.**
What do you think about . . . ?

_____ **Repeat for clarification.**

José and Carlos are having a party.

🔲 **Listen and read.**

● ● ● ● ● ● ● ● ● ● ● ● ● ● ● ● ● ● ●

Ms. Apple: Students, José and Carlos want to talk to you.

José: We're having a party to celebrate the end of the school term and our new home. It's a housewarming.

Carlos: It's on Friday night at our new house. Here's a map. It's a potluck.

José: We're also celebrating Carlos' family moving to the USA.

Why are José and Carlos talking to the class?

🔲 **Listen and read. Guess the best answer and circle the letter. Check your work on page 170.**

1. "Celebrating" means
    a. having a good time.
    b. having a test.

2. End of school "term" means
    a. the end of school.
    b. doing homework.

3. "Housewarming" means
    a. a party at a new home.
    b. a fire at a home.

4. "Potluck" means
    a. pots and pans.
    b. bringing food to a party.

A celebration!

Listen and read.

1. A potluck is a party to which everyone brings food.

2. A housewarming is a celebration for a new home. Everyone usually brings a small gift for the house.

3. The end of the school term is the time when classes are over. We say good-bye to our class and teacher.

4. A celebration is having a good time at a potluck, housewarming, or end of the school term.

When do you have it?

Write the words.

| potluck | celebration | end of school term | housewarming |

a. It's a _____.
We take gifts for the house.

b. It's the _____. We say
good-bye to the class and to the teacher.

c. It's a _____.
We take food.

d. All of these people are having
a _____.

 Practice.

What are some other celebrations?

What are some
other celebrations?

In my country we
celebrate _____.

_____

_____

_____

_____

_____

_____

What year is it?

Make a calendar for this year.
Ask your teacher for help.

Year: _____

JANUARY						
S	M	T	W	Th	F	S

FEBRUARY						
S	M	T	W	Th	F	S

MARCH						
S	M	T	W	Th	F	S

APRIL						
S	M	T	W	Th	F	S

MAY						
S	M	T	W	Th	F	S

JUNE						
S	M	T	W	Th	F	S

JULY						
S	M	T	W	Th	F	S

AUGUST						
S	M	T	W	Th	F	S

SEPTEMBER						
S	M	T	W	Th	F	S

OCTOBER						
S	M	T	W	Th	F	S

NOVEMBER						
S	M	T	W	Th	F	S

DECEMBER						
S	M	T	W	Th	F	S

Circle the dates of the celebrations you find on the next page.

What other celebrations?

 Find the dates on this year's calendar with your teacher. Write the date under the picture.

1. New Year's Day

Date: _January 1_

2. Martin Luther King, Jr.'s Birthday

Date: _____

3. Hanukkah

Date: _____

4. Ramadan

Date: _____

5. Presidents' Day

Date: _____

6. Valentine's Day

Date: _____

7. Chinese New Year Têt

Date: _____

8. Easter

Date: _____

9. Memorial Day

Date: _____

10. Independence Day

Date: _____

11. Veterans Day

Date: _____

12. Halloween

Date: _____

13. Columbus Day

Date: _____

14. Thanksgiving

Date: _____

15. Labor Day

Date: _____

16. Christmas

Date: _____

José and his family go shopping for party food.

 Listen and read.

José, Carlos, and their families are getting ready for the party. Carlos and his wife, Maria, are cleaning the new house. José, his wife, Carlotta, and their daughter, Juanita, are going shopping for food. Help them with their shopping list.

 Write.

Shopping List	
_____	_____
_____	_____
_____	_____
_____	_____
_____	_____

It's your choice.

🔲 **Listen and read.**

What foods do people take to parties?

1. chips

2. juice

3. tortillas

4. salsa

5. egg rolls

6. sushi

7. pita bread

8. hot dogs

9. pizza

10. salad

11. meat and rice

12. sandwiches

🔲 ✎ **Listen and underline the words you hear.**

✎ **Write. What do you take to parties?**

_____   _____   _____

_____   _____   _____

_____   _____   _____

Let's get ready!

shaving

brushing teeth

taking a shower

getting dressed

combing hair

Listen and write.

Grandpa is getting ready for the party.

1. He is ———— a ————, 2. ———— his ———— 3. and ———————.

4. He is ————————— 5. and ———— his ————.

When he is ready, he takes his food for the potluck, reads his map to the party, and walks to the bus stop.

Are you ready yet?

Match the word with the picture.

1.

2.

3.

4.

5.

a. shaving

b. brushing teeth

c. getting dressed

d. combing hair

e. taking a shower

Write the words under the picture.

1. _shaving_

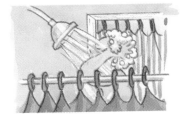

2. _____

3. _____

4. _____

5. _____

School is out!

Listen and read.

Ms. Apple is very happy and pleased to be giving all the students their end of the term certificates.

Sue: Stop the music! Stop dancing for a minute. Come here. I want to give you something.

José: Everyone come to the living room. Ms. Apple wants to talk to us.

Sue: I want to congratulate all of you. We are at the end of the school term. You finished the class. You have learned English and have also made many new friends. Good luck to you all. Here is a certificate for each of you.

Certificate of Completion

This is to certify that

_____

has successfully completed

_____

level of class

_____

name of class

on

_____

date

at _____

name of school

_____   _____

date   signature

I can do this.

_____ Understand cultural concepts of housewarming, potluck, and end of school term.

_____ Understand the cultural concept of preparing for a party or celebration.

_____ Understand the significance of certificate of completion.

_____ Read and mark dates on a calendar.

_____ Identify holidays, special dates, celebrations, and their significance.

_____ Identify foods from different cultures.

chips	juice	tortillas	salsa
egg rolls	sushi	pita bread	hot dogs
pizza	salad	meat and rice	sandwiches

_____ Identify basic grooming habits and activities.

shaving	brushing teeth	taking a shower
getting dressed	combing hair	

_____ Write a shopping list.

Note: When it is possible to provide answers, they are given in italics.

Page 2 *How are you?*
Listen and read.

Ms. Apple:	How are you this morning?
Petra:	I'm great!
Ms. Apple:	Great?
Petra:	Yes, great!
	Point to *great.*
Ms. Apple:	How are you this afternoon?
Alicia:	Fine!
Ms. Apple:	Fine?
Alicia:	Yes, fine.
	Point to *fine.*
Ms. Apple:	How are you this evening?
Mr. Duval:	I'm so-so.
Ms. Apple:	Just so-so?
Mr. Duval:	Yeah, just so-so.
	Point to *so-so.*
Ms. Apple:	How are you this morning?
Farima:	Good!
Ms. Apple:	Good?
Farima:	Yes, I'm good this morning.
	Point to *good.*
Farima:	How are you this afternoon?
Ms. Apple:	I'm happy!
Farima:	Really happy?
Ms. Apple:	Yes, really happy.
	Point to *happy.*

Page 4 *How are you feeling?*
Listen and read.

Ms. Apple:	How are you feeling this morning?
Makeba:	I'm sad.
Ms. Apple:	Sad?
Makeba:	Yes, sad!
	Point to *sad.*
Ms. Apple:	How are you this afternoon?
Farima:	I'm bored.
Ms. Apple:	Bored?
Farima:	Yeah, I'm bored.
	Point to *bored.*
Ms. Apple:	How are you this evening?
Van Ly:	Sick!
Ms. Apple:	Sick?
Van Ly:	Yes, sick.
	Point to *sick.*
Ms. Apple:	How are you this morning?
Mrs. Said:	I'm angry.
Ms. Apple:	Really angry?
Mrs. Said:	Yeah, really angry.
	Point to *angry.*
Ms. Apple:	How are you this afternoon?
Carlos:	Upset!
Ms. Apple:	Upset?
Carlos:	Yes, I'm upset this afternoon.
	Point to *upset.*
Ms. Apple:	How are you this evening?
José:	I'm tired!
Ms. Apple:	Really tired?
José:	Yes, tired.
	Point to *tired.*

Page 5 *Do you remember?*
Listen and circle the letter you hear.

1. **Teacher:** Please circle *v.*
   Student: *V* as in *vacation*?
   Teacher: Yes, *v.* Please circle *v.*
2. **Teacher:** Please circle *e.*
   Student: *E*?
   Teacher: Yes, *e.* Please circle *e.*
3. **Teacher:** Please circle *e.*
   Student: *I* or *e*?
   Teacher: *E.* Please circle *e.*
4. **Teacher:** Please circle *s.*
   Student: *S* as in *say*?
   Teacher: Yes, *s.* Please circle *s.*
5. **Teacher:** Please circle *g.*
   Student: *G* or *j*?
   Teacher: *G* as in *great.* Please circle *g.*
6. **Teacher:** Please circle *s.*
   Student: *S* or *x*?
   Teacher: *S* as in *so-so.* Please circle *s.*
7. **Teacher:** Please circle *a.*
   Student: *A* or *i*?
   Teacher: *A.* Please circle *a.*
8. **Teacher:** Please circle *n.*
   Student: *M* as in *morning* or *n* as in *no*?
   Teacher: *N* as in *no.* Please circle *n.*
9. **Teacher:** Please circle *y.*
   Student: *Y* or *i* ?
   Teacher: *Y* as in *yes.* Please circle *y.*

Now listen and circle the number you hear.

1. **Teacher:** Please circle *13.*
   Student: *13* or *30*?
   Teacher: *13.* Please circle *13.*
2. **Teacher:** Please circle *22.*
   Student: *2* or *22*?
   Teacher: *22.* Please circle *22.*
3. **Teacher:** Please circle *12.*
   Student: *12* or *13*?
   Teacher: *12.* Please circle *12.*
4. **Teacher:** Please circle *4.*
   Student: *4* or *14*?
   Teacher: *4.* Please circle *4.*
5. **Teacher:** Please circle *6.*
   Student: *6* or *16*?
   Teacher: *6.* Please circle *6.*
6. **Teacher:** Please circle *29.*
   Student: *29, 9,* or *19*?
   Teacher: *29.* Please circle *29.*
7. **Teacher:** Please circle *28.*
   Student: *8, 18,* or *28*?
   Teacher: *28.* Please circle *28.*
8. **Teacher:** Please circle *30.*
   Student: *30* or *13*?
   Teacher: *30.* Please circle *30.*
9. **Teacher:** Please circle *17.*
   Student: *17* or *7*?
   Teacher: *17.* Please circle *17.*

Listen and write the missing letters.

Look above #3. Write the letter *e.* Write the letter *e.*
Look above #4. Write the letter *a.* Write the letter *a.*
Look above #7. Write the letter *t.* Write the letter *t.*
Look above #9. Write the letter *d.* Write the letter *d.*

Look above #12. Write the letter *t*. Write the letter *t*.
Answer: *great student*

Page 6   *This is our classroom.*
Listen and point.
1. **board.** Do you see the board? Point to the board.
2. **calendar.** Look by the board for the calendar. Point to the calendar.
3. **computer.** Can you use the computer? Point to the computer.
4. **flag.** Can you find the flag? Point to the flag.
5. **map.** The map is over the calendar. Point to the map.
6. **clock.** Look over the door to find the clock. Point to the clock.
7. **bookcase.** The bookcase is under the flag. Point to the bookcase.
8. **projector.** Ask your teacher for help to find the projector. Point to the projector.
9. **wheelchair.** The teacher is in the wheelchair. Point to the wheelchair.
10. **calculator.** Do you see the student with a calculator? Point to the calculator.
11. **pencil sharpener.** Look by the door for the pencil sharpener. Point to the pencil sharpener.
12. **screen.** The screen is over the board. Point to the screen.

Page 7   *Is this a clock?*
Listen and circle.
1. Look at A. Is this the clock? Is A the clock? *no*
2. Look at B. Is this the calendar? Is B the calendar? *yes*
3. Look at C. Is this the map? Is C the map? *yes*
4. Look at D. Is this the board? Is D the board? *yes*
5. Look at E. Is this the bookcase? Is E the bookcase? *no*
6. Look at F. Is this the projector? Is F the projector? *yes*
7. Look at G. Is this the calculator? Is G the calculator? *no*
8. Look at H. Is this the clock? Is H the clock? *yes*
9. Look at I. Is this the screeen? Is I the screen? *no*

10. Look at J. Is this the computer? Is J the computer? *no*
11. Look at K. Is this the wheelchair? Is K the wheelchair? *yes*
12. Look at L. Is this the map? Is L the map? *no*

Page 9   *Male? Female?*
Listen, read, and write.

Look at A.	This is a male. What letter goes on the line?
	Ms. Apple: Write *M* on the line.
Look at B.	This is a female. What letter goes on the line?
	Ms. Apple: Write *F* on the line.
Look at C.	This is a single male. He isn't married. What letter goes on the line?
	Ms. Apple: Write *S* for single.
Look at D.	This is a single female. She isn't married. What letter goes on the line?
Ms. Apple:	Write *S* for single.
Student:	Write *S* for both male and female?
Ms. Apple:	Yes, write *S* for both.
Look at E.	The couple is married.
Student:	Do I write *M*?
Ms. Apple:	Yes, write *M*.
Look at F.	The couple is divorced. They aren't married now.
Student:	Do I write *D*?
Ms. Apple:	Yes, write *D*.

Page 11   Review.
Listen and circle.
1. She is so **sad**. Look for the sad person. Circle the letter. *b*
2. Grandpa is so **sick**. Look for the sick person. Circle the letter. *a*
3. Farima's mother is so **angry**. Look for the angry person. Circle the letter. *b*
4. Carlos is **tired** today. Look for the tired person. Circle the letter. *a*

STUDENT BOOK   **TAPESCRIPT**   **UNIT 2**   *There is no school on Saturday.*

Page 15   *Look at the week.*
Listen and read.

Sunday.	The first day is Sunday. No school on Sunday. Read *Sunday*.
Monday.	The next day is Monday. This is a school day and a work day. Read *Monday*.
Tuesday.	The day after Monday is Tuesday. Read *Tuesday*.
Wednesday.	It's Wednesday. Read *Wednesday*.
Thursday.	Then, it's Thursday. Read *Thursday*.
Friday.	Usually, the last school day and workday is Friday. Read *Friday*.
Saturday.	Saturday is a great day. What do you do on Saturday? Read *Saturday*.

Page 16   Review.
Listen and read.
1. **exercise.** I exercise on Monday, Wednesday, and Friday. Read *exercise*. Find the picture.
2. **rest.** Sunday is my day to rest. Read *rest*. Find the picture.

3. **dance.** We dance every Friday night. Read *dance*. Find the picture.
4. **go to school.** On Monday, I go to school. Read *go to school*. Find the picture.
5. **shop.** Teacher: Do you like to shop?
      Student: Shop?
      Teacher: Yes, shop.
      Student: Of course, I love to shop.
   Read *shop*. Find the picture.
6. **go to work.** Student: I go to work on Saturdays.
      Teacher: Work?
      Student: Yes, I go to work on Saturdays.
   Read *go to work*. Find the picture.

Page 18   *What time is it?*
Listen and check the time you hear.
1. **twelve-fifteen.** Let's eat lunch. It's twelve-fifteen. Make a check under twelve-fifteen. *b*
2. **twelve-thirty.** My clock says twelve-thirty. Make a check under twelve-thirty. *b*

3. **ten o'clock.** Want some coffee? It's ten o'clock. Check ten o'clock. *a*
4. **six o'clock.** It's six o'clock. Time for the six o'clock news. Check six o'clock. *a*
5. **two-thirty.** Class is over. Time to go. It's two-thirty. Check two-thirty. *b*
6. **eight-fifteen.** Good evening. It's eight-fifteen. Check eight-fifteen. *b*

Page 19   Please turn on the lamp.
Listen and point.
1. **A: lamp.** Please turn on the lamp.
   B: The lamp on the table?
   A: Yes, that one. Point to the lamp.
2. **A: door.** Is someone at the door?
   B: At the door? No, there is no one at the door.
   A: Point to the door.
3. **A: sofa.** I really like my sofa.
   B: The big sofa?
   A: Yes, the big sofa. Point to the sofa.
4. **A: calendar.** Where is the calendar?
   B: Next to the clock.
   A: Oh, I see it. Point to the calendar.
5. **A: rug.** Don't trip on the rug.
   B: Don't worry. I won't trip on the rug.
   A: Point to the rug.

6. **A: floor.** Look near the door. The rug is on the floor.
   B: Near the door? On the floor?
   A: Yep. The rug on the floor. Point to the floor.
7. **A: picture.** The picture is new. Do you like it?
   B: The picture? Oh, yes. I love the new picture.
   A: Point to the picture.
8. **A: wall.** The new picture is on the wall.
   B: Which wall?
   A: The wall behind the sofa. Point to the wall.
9. **A: television.** In the evening, do you watch television?
   B: Sure, at night I watch television.
   A: Point to the television.
10. **A: chair.** Is there only one chair?
    B: Only one chair? No, there are four chairs.
    A: Point to one chair.
11. **A: table.** Where is the table?
    B: Table? Isn't it next to the chairs?
    A: Yes, next to the chairs is the table. Point to the table.
12. **A: window.** Where is the window?
    B: The window?
    A: Yes, the window. Point to the window.

STUDENT BOOK   UNIT 3
TAPESCRIPT

Can we buy some ice cream?

Page 26   Where's the ice cream?
Listen, find the picture, and read the word.
1. **cake**   Do you see the cake? Find the cake. Read *cake*.
2. **bread**   Where is the bread? Find the bread. Read *bread*.
3. **rice**   Is there some rice? Find the rice. Read *rice*.
4. **pasta**   The pasta is next to the rice. Find the pasta. Read *pasta*.
5. **flour**   I need some flour. Find the flour. Read *flour*.
6. **coffee**   Do you drink coffee? Find the coffee. Read *coffee*.
7. **tea**   I like tea very much. Find the tea. Read *tea*.
8. **soda**   She drinks soda. Find the soda. Read *soda*.
9. **salt**   Where is the salt? Find the salt. Read *salt*.
10. **sugar**   Do you use sugar? Find the sugar. Read *sugar*.
11. **fish**   I want to buy some fish. Find the fish. Read *fish*.
12. **beef**   Where's the beef? Find the beef. Read *beef*.
13. **pork**   She doesn't eat pork. Find the pork. Read *pork*.
14. **chicken**   He needs a chicken. Find the chicken. Read *chicken*.
15. **cabbage**   I like cabbage a lot. Find the cabbage. Read *cabbage*.
16. **broccoli**   Kathy doesn't like broccoli. Find the broccoli. Read *broccoli*.
17. **juice**   What kind of juice do you like? Find the juice. Read *juice*.
18. **ice cream**   Kathy loves ice cream. Find the ice cream. Read *ice cream*.
19. **milk**   Drink a lot of milk. Find the milk. Read *milk*.
20. **butter**   Where's the butter? Find the butter. Read *butter*.

Page 27   Where are the oranges?
Listen and read the food words.
1. **cookies**   I love cookies, don't you? Find the cookies. Read *cookies*.
2. **noodles**   She buys noodles at the store. Find the noodles. Read *noodles*.
3. **oranges**   Oranges are so good. Find the oranges. Read *oranges*.
4. **peaches**   Where are the peaches? Find the peaches. Read *peaches*.
5. **bananas**   Do you see the bananas? Find the bananas. Read *bananas*.
6. **potatoes**   Do you want one potato or three potatoes? Find the potatoes. Read *potatoes*.
7. **beans**   Can you count the beans? Find the beans. Read *beans*.
8. **carrots**   He doesn't like carrots. Find the carrots. Read *carrots*.
9. **sodas**   She can drink many sodas. Find the sodas. Read *sodas*.
10. **chickens**   Do you see the two chickens. Do you? Find the chickens. Read *chickens*.

Page 28   Review.
Listen and circle the words you hear.
1. I want to buy some noodles. Circle the noodles. *b*
2. Do you have cookies? Circle the cookies. *b*
3. I like cake. Circle the cake. *a*
4. We eat fish for dinner. Circle the fish. *c*
5. Bananas are great! Circle the bananas. *c*

Listen, look at the picture, and circle *Yes* or *No*.

1. Look at 1. Is this tea? Circle *Yes* or *No*. Yes
2. Look at 2. Is this fish? Circle *Yes* or *No*. No
3. Look at 3. Is this sugar? Circle *Yes* or *No*. No
4. Look at 4. Is this flour? Circle *Yes* or *No*. Yes
5. Look at 5. Is this bread? Circle *Yes* or *No*. Yes
6. Look at 6. Are these noodles? Circle *Yes* or *No*. No
7. Look at 7. Is this a chicken? Circle *Yes* or *No*. Yes
8. Look at 8. Is this an apple? Circle *Yes* or *No*. No
9. Look at 9. Is this beef? Circle *Yes* or *No*. No
10. Look at 10. Is this pork? Circle *Yes* or *No*. Yes
11. Look at 11. Is this coffee? Circle *Yes* or *No*. Yes
12. Look at 12. Is this sugar? Circle *Yes* or *No*. Yes

Listen and point.

A: This is a penny.
B: A penny?
A: Yes, a penny. Find the penny.
B: This is a nickel.
C: A nickel?
B: Yes, a nickel. Find the nickel.
C: This is a dime.
D: A dime?
C: Yes, a dime. Find the dime.
D: This is a quarter.
A: A quarter?
D: Yes, a quarter. Find the quarter.
A: This is a half dollar.
B: A half dollar?
A: Yes, a half dollar. Find the half dollar.
B: This is a one-dollar bill. Find the one-dollar bill.
C: This is a five-dollar bill. Find the five-dollar bill.
D: This is a ten-dollar bill. Find the ten-dollar bill.
A: This is a twenty-dollar bill. Find the twenty-dollar bill.

Listen and circle the amount you hear.

1. **Teacher:** Twelve dollars and seventy-five cents.
   Student: Did you say twelve dollars and seventy-five cents?
   Teacher: That's right. Circle twelve dollars and seventy-five cents. *b*
2. **Teacher:** I need two-ten for the taxi.
   Student: Do you mean two dollars and ten cents?
   Teacher: Sure. Circle two dollars and ten cents. *a*
3. **Teacher:** Fifty dollars and seventy-three cents is the price of the dress.
   Student: Fifty seventy-three?
   Teacher: Yes. Circle fifty dollars and seventy-three cents. *a*
4. **Teacher:** I want to borrow seventeen dollars.
   Student: Do you want seventeen dollars?
   Teacher: That's right. Circle seventeen dollars. *c*
5. **Teacher:** She needs three seventy-five.
   Student: Is that three dollars and seventy-five cents?
   Teacher: Yep. Circle three seventy-five. *c*
6. **Teacher:** Do you have twenty-five dollars and forty-four cents?
   Student: Twenty-five dollars and forty-four cents?
   Teacher: That's correct. Circle twenty-five dollars and forty-four cents. *c*
7. **Teacher:** The food costs fifty dollars.
   Student: Only fifty dollars?
   Teacher: Yes, circle fifty dollars. *b*
8. **Teacher:** The rice costs one fifteen.
   Student: Is that one dollar and fifteen cents?

Teacher: That's right! Circle one fifteen. *a*

Listen and write the amount you hear.

1. **A:** Do you have $15.42?
   B: $15.42?
   A: That's right. Do you have $15.42? Write $15.42.
2. **A:** The oranges cost $2.10.
   B: $2.10?
   A: Yep. $2.10. The oranges cost $2.10. Write $2.10.
3. **A:** She has $50.00.
   B: She has only $50.00?
   A: Correct. She has only $50.00. Write $50.00.
4. **A:** He has $17.50.
   B: Are you sure he has $17.50, not $70.50?
   A: I'm sure. He has $17.50. Write $17.50.
5. **A:** Do you have a ten-dollar bill?
   B: Do you mean ten dollars?
   A: Yes, a ten-dollar bill is ten dollars. Write ten dollars.
6. **A:** The meat costs $4.95.
   B: I think the meat costs $4.85.
   A: No, you're wrong. The meat costs $4.95. Write $4.95.
7. **A:** Bic gave Kim $4.85.
   B: Bic gave Kim $4.95?
   A: No, not $4.95, $4.85. Write $4.85.
8. **A:** Grandpa gave Grandma $700.00.
   B: Are you sure it's $700.00?
   A: I'm sure it's $700. Write $700.
9. **A:** Can you buy a TV for $100.00.
   B: No, I can't buy one for $100.00. Can you?
   A: Yes, a small one costs $100.00. Write $100.
10. **A:** I have a new chair. It cost $21.43.
    B: $21.43 or $21.23?
    A: My new chair cost $21.43. Write $21.43.

Listen and circle the amount you hear.

1. **A nickel**. One apple costs a nickel. Circle the nickel.
2. **A quarter**. Show me the quarter. Circle the quarter.
3. **Twenty cents.** Bic has twenty cents in his pocket. Circle twenty cents.
4. **Ten cents.** Ten cents is a dime. Circle ten cents.

Circle the amount you hear.

1. **A:** The sodas cost two dollars and ninety-five cents.
   B: The sodas cost three dollars and ninety-five cents?
   A: No, they cost two dollars and ninety-five cents. Circle two ninety-five. *b*
2. **A:** The rice costs one-o-one.
   B: The sodas cost one-o-one?
   A: No, that's wrong. The rice costs one-o-one. Circle one-o-one. *c*
3. **A:** I spent two forty-nine.
   B: Two forty-nine or three forty nine?
   A: Two forty-nine. Circle two forty-nine. *a*
4. **A:** The cookies cost one dollar and fifty-one cents.
   B: The cookies cost one dollar and fifteen cents?
   A: No, they cost one dollar and fifty-one cents. Circle one-fifty-one. *c*
5. **A:** What can you buy for ninety-five cents?
   B: You can buy three oranges for ninety-five cents.
   A: Circle ninety-five cents. *c*
6. **A:** Can you buy beef for six ninety-five?
   B: You can buy chicken for six ninety-five. One chicken for six ninety-five. *a*

Page 44   Review.

Listen.   Listen and write the word.

A: sofa. José has a sofa in his living room.
B: Did you say *sofa*?
A: Yes, José has a sofa in his living room.   Write *sofa*.

A: sink.   Do you see the sink?
B: Do you mean the sink in the kitchen or the one in the bathroom?
A: The bathroom sink.   Write *sink*.

A: toilet.   Where is the toilet?
B: Silly, the toilet is in the bathroom.
A: I know, the toilet is in the bathroom.   Write *toilet*.

A: cabinet.   Is the food in the cabinet?
B: The cabinet in the kitchen?   Yes, the food is in the cabinet.   Write *cabinet*.

A: shower.   I need to use the shower.
B: Okay, it's in the bathroom.
A: I know the shower is in the bathroom.   Write *shower*.

A: dresser.   Do you have a dresser?
B: Sure, there's a dresser in my bedroom.
A: I want to use your dresser.   Write *dresser*.

A: microwave.   Can you find the microwave?
B: Yep, the microwave is in the kitchen.
A: I agree, the microwave is usually in the kitchen.   Write *microwave*.

A: refrigerator.   Is the refrigerator usually in the kitchen?
B: Of course, the refrigerator is usually in the kitchen.

A: Can you find the refrigerator in the kitchen?   Write *refrigerator*.

A: lamp.   Can you turn on the lamp?
B: The lamp in the bedroom or in the living room?
A: The lamp in the bedroom.   Write *lamp*.

A: stove.   Where is the stove?
B: I don't see the stove.
A: It's in the kitchen.   Write *stove*.

A: tub.   Do you have a tub in your bathroom?
B: Sure, I have a tub in my bathroom.
A: Oh, I see the tub in your bathroom.   Write *tub*.

A: bed.   Where is the bed?
B: Now, where do you think the bed is?
A: Oh, I see the bed.   Write *bed*.

A: table.   Is there a table in the living room?
B: Yep, there surely is a table in the living room.
A: Is the table near the chair?   Write *table*.

A: picture. There is a picture on the wall.
B: A picture?
A: That's right.   There is a picture on the wall.   Write *picture*.

A: television. Where's the television?
B: The television is in the living room, too.
A: Oh, I see the television.   Write *television*.

A: night stand.   Where is the night stand?
B: The night stand?
A: Yes, the night stand.
B: The night stand is in my bedroom next to my bed.   Write *night stand*.

Page 51   What color is the coat?

Look, listen, and point.

Find women's clothes.
Point to the red dress.   Red dress.
Point to the yellow blouse.   Yellow blouse.
Point to the purple purse.   Purple purse.
Point to the black sandals.   Black sandals.
Point to the white underwear. White underwear.
Point to the brown skirt.   Brown skirt.
Point again and say the word.
Find children's clothes.
Point to the blue and white socks. Blue and white socks.
Point to the white tennis shoes.   White tennis shoes.
Point to the blue cap.   Blue cap.
Point to the orange T-shirt.   Orange T-shirt.
Point to the yellow shorts.   Yellow shorts.
Point again and say the word.
Find the men's clothes.
Point to the blue suit.   Blue suit.
Point to the red sweater.   Red sweater.
Point to the white shirt.   White shirt.
Point to the green tie.   Green tie.
Point to the gray pants.   Gray pants.
Point to the brown men's shoes.   Brown men's shoes.
Point to the black hat.   Black hat.
Point again and say the word.

Listen and write.
1. Find the coat.   What color is the coat?   Is it green or brown?
2. Find the socks.   What color are the socks?   Are they green and yellow or are they blue and white?
3. Find the shirt and tie.   What color are the shirt and tie?   Is the shirt white or gray?   Is the tie green or blue?
4. Find the pants.   What color are the pants?   Are they gray or brown?
5. Find the T-shirt.   What color is the T-shirt?   Is it orange or purple?
6. Find the sweater.   What color is the sweater?   Is it purple or red?
7. Can you find a blue cap?   In which department?
8. Can you find black sandals?   In which department?
9. Can you find a suit?   In which department?

Page 57   I'm so happy!

Listen and repeat.
I'm surprised.   I'm excited.   I'm thrilled.

Page 59   Review.

Listen and circle the same amount.
1. The tennis shoes cost twenty dollars and twenty-five cents. *a*
2. The T-shirt costs seven twenty-five. *b*
3. Can you buy the socks for only one fifty? *a*

4. Her dress cost twenty-one thirty-five. *c*

Listen and make a check on the amount you hear.
1. She's selling the purple purse for fifteen-fifteen. *a*
2. Isn't forty dollars and twenty-six cents too much for a blouse? *b*

3. The dress is cheap. It's only thirteen-thirty. *a*
4. The red sweater is expensive. It's seventy sixty-seven. *a*

STUDENT BOOK
TAPESCRIPT **UNIT 6**

We are having a yard sale. Can you come?

Page 62 Look at José's map.
Listen and find the place on the map.
1. **School.** Find Duttonville School. Take your time. Find Duttonville School.
2. **A:** **Park.** We walk in the park every Sunday.
   B: You walk in the park every Sunday?
   A: Sure, every Sunday we walk in the park. Find the park.
3. **A:** **Market.** I need to buy my food at the market.
   B: The market near Grand Avenue?
   C: Yes, I need to buy food at that market. Find the market.
4. **Post office.** Do you see the post office? Find the post office on First Street.
5. **Church.** Can you find the church? It's on Main Street. Find the church.
6. **A:** **Bus stop.** Is the bus stop next to the post office?
   B: No, the bus stop is across the street from the post office.
   A: Oh, I see the bus stop. Find the bus stop.
7. **Movie theater.** I'll meet you at the movie theater. Find the movie theater.
8. **Bank.** Where is the bank? Take your time. Find the bank.

Find these on the page.
left. Point to the policewoman who is saying "Go left." Read *left*.
right. Point to the policeman who is saying "Go right." Read *right*.

Page 63 How can I get from Duttonville School to the park?
Look, listen, and read.
A. walk. Walk across the street.
B: Walk or run?
A: Walk across the street. Read *walk*.
B: go straight. Find "Go straight."
A: Read *go straight*.
B: go left. Hold out your left hand and go left.
C: Go left?
B: Yes, go left. Read *go left*.
C: go right. Hold out your right hand and go right.
B: Go right?
C: Correct. Go right.
A: Beside means next to. Read *beside*.
A: across from. Do you remember **across from**? Read *across from*.
B: on the corner. Find the house on the corner.
A: between. The street is between the trees in the park. Find the picture that shows, "Between." Read *between*.

Page 65 Pots and pans.
Look, listen, and write the number in the circle.
1. **C:** **Broom.** The broom is next to the chair.
   A: Find the broom.
   C: Point to the broom. Write number 1 in the circle.
2. **C:** **Coffee pot.** Can I buy a coffee pot?
   B: Sure. There's a coffee pot on the ironing board.
   C: Oh, I see it. I want to buy the coffee pot. Write #2 in the circle.
3. **D:** **Dishes.** Find the dishes.
   A: They're on the table next to the glasses.
   D: Where are the dishes? Write #3 in the circle.
4. **D:** **Dryer.** So, is the dryer next to the washer?
   C: Of course, the washer and dryer are next to each other.
   D: I see the dryer. Can you find the dryer?
5. **C:** **Glasses.** The glasses are on the table next to the dishes.
   B: Are the glasses next to the pots and pans?
   C: No. The glasses are on the table next to the dishes. See the glasses?
6. **B:** **Iron.** Is there an iron?
   C: Yes, the iron is on the ironing board.
   B: Oh, there's the iron.
7. **D:** **Ironing board.** Where is the ironing board?
   B: The ironing board is in front of the washer and dryer.
   D: I see the ironing board.
8. **C:** **Pots and pans.** Can you find the pots and pans?
   A: Pots and pans?
   C: Yes, pots and pans.
9. **C:** **Tea kettle.** The tea kettle is next to the rug.
   B: You say the tea kettle is next to the rug?
   C: That's right. There's the tea kettle.
10. **A:** Her dad needs some ties. Do you have ties?
    C: Of course we do. The ties are next to the jacket.
    A: Sure, there are the ties.
11. **C:** **Toaster.** Do you see the toaster?
    D: Yes, the toaster is under the table.
    C: Oh, yeah. the toaster is under the table. Can you find the toaster?
12. **B:** **Trash can.** Is there a trash can for sale?
    A: Yes, there is a trash can near the clothes.
    B: Oh, I see the trash can.
13. **C:** **Vacuum.** The vacuum is on the grass.
    D: Yes, the vacuum is on the grass. Is it next to the chair?
    C: No, the vacuum is in front of the pots and pans. Do you see the vacuum.
14. **D:** **Washer.** The washer and dryer are next to each other.
    C: The washer is next to the dryer? Oh, I see the washer.

Listen and write the letter on the line.
1. **A:** I want to buy a rug.
   B: The one next to the tea kettle?
   A: No, I want to buy the rug under the table.
   Write the letter of the rug under the table.
2. **A:** He is buying the lamp.
   B: The lamp next to the books?
   A: No, the lamp on the table.
   Write the letter of the lamp on the table.
3. **A:** She wants the blue dress.
   B: The blue dress next to the blouse?
   A: Yes, next to the blouse and over the red dress.
   Write the letter of the blue dress.
4. **A:** How much is the sofa?
   B: The sofa? It's twenty-five dollars.
   Write the letter of the sofa.
5. **A:** My mother needs a chair.
   B: Do you like the one next to the sofa?
   A: Yes. I'll buy that chair.

6. **B:** What about books? Do you want any books?
   A: Actually, I do. I want to buy the books beside the lamp.
   B: The books on the table?
   A: No, the books beside the lamp.
7. **A:** I want a table.
   B: Which one do you like?
   A: I like the one with the lamp and dishes on it.
8. **A:** My father wants a coat.
   B: The brown one or the blue one?
   A: The blue coat.
9. **A:** Van Ly is buying the tea kettle.
   B: Did you say tea kettle or coffee pot?
   A: I said tea kettle.

**S T U D E N T   B O O K
T A P E S C R I P T**

**U N I T
7**

This is an emergency!

Listen and underline these words in the story.
1. **Emergency.** "He says, This is an emergency." Emergency.
2. **Rain.** It's starting to rain. Rain.
3. **Leave.** José and Van Ly leave the yard sale. Leave.
4. **Crossing.** A man is crossing the street. Crossing.
5. **Street.** A man is crossing the street. Street.
6. **Fast.** A car is going very fast. Fast.
7. **Hits.** A car is going very fast and hits Carlos. Hits.
8. **Runs.** José runs to call 911. Runs.
9. **Call.** José runs to call 911. Call.
10. **911.** José runs to call 911. 911.
11. **Report.** José runs to call 911 and report the traffic accident. Report.
12. **Traffic accident.** José runs to call 911 and report the traffic accident. Traffic accident.

Read and talk about the underlined words.

Listen and read the word.
1. **Drowning.** Help! A man is drowning! Read *drowning.*
2. **Bleeding.** His leg is bleeding. Read *bleeding.*
3. **Choking.** Come quick! The woman is choking. Read *choking.*
4. **Traffic accident.** Call 911! There's a traffic accident. Read *traffic accident.*
5. **Robbery.** Call the police! There's a robbery. Read *robbery.*
6. **Fire.** Call the fire department. The house is on fire. Read *fire.*

Listen and match the words with the pictures.
1. **Drowning.** Help! A man is drowning! Find the word and write the number one. drowning.
2. **Choking.** Come quick! The woman is choking. Find the word and write the number two. choking.
3. **Robbery.** Call the police. There's a robbery. Find the word and write the number three. robbery

4. **Bleeding.** His leg is bleeding. Find the word and write the number four. bleeding.
5. **Traffic accident.** Call 911. There is a traffic accident. Find the words and write the number five. traffic accident.
6. **Fire.** Call the fire department. The house is on fire. Find the word and write the number six. fire.

Listen and read.
1. **A:** **Raining.** I'm wet! It's raining. Read *raining.*
2. **B:** **Snowing**: Br-r-r-r. It's so cold that it's snowing. Read *snowing.*
3. **A:** **Sunny.** The sun is shining. It's sunny. Read *sunny.*
4. **B:** **Cloudy.** The sun is not shining. It's cloudy. Read *cloudy.*
5. **A:** **Windy.** Look at the tree. It's so windy today. Read *windy.*
6. **B:** **Foggy.** I can't see. It's so foggy. Read *foggy.*
7. **A.** **Hot.** Whew! I'm so hot! Read *hot.*
8. **B:** **Cold.** Br-r-r-r. It's snowing. It's very cold. Read *cold.*

Listen and read.
1. **A:** **Hospital.** They are taking Carlos to the hospital. Read *hospital.*
2. **B:** **Medical Form.** Carlos is filling out the medical form. Read *medical form.*
3. **A:** **Nurse.** The doctor and nurse meet Carlos. Read *nurse.*
4. **B:** **Doctor.** The woman is the doctor. Read *doctor.*
5. **A:** **Patient.** Carlos is a patient at the hospital. Read *patient.*
6. **B:** **Paramedics.** The paramedics help Carlos. Read *paramedics.*
7. **A:** **Ambulance.** They take Carlos to the hospital in the ambulance. Read *ambulance.*
8. **B:** **Emergency room.** The doctor and nurse meet Carlos at the door of the emergency room. Read *emergency room.*

Page 82 *What's the matter with Carlos?*
Listen and read.

A: Head. Put your finger on the man's head. Nod your head. Read *head*.

B: Neck. Put your finger on the man's neck. Stretch your neck. Read *neck*.

A: Chest. Put your finger on the man's chest. Pat your chest. Read *chest*.

A: Arm. Put your finger on the man's arm. Wave your arm. Read *arm*.

B: Hand. Put your finger on the man's hand. Raise your hand. Read *hand*.

A: Leg. Put your finger on the man's leg. Shake your leg. Read *leg*.

B: Foot. Put your finger on the man's foot. Stamp your foot. Read *foot*.

A: Back. Put your finger on the man's back. Pat your classmate on the back. Read *back*.

Somebody is sick with a cold.

Page 86 *What's the matter?*
First listen. Then, listen and write.

1. **A: sick.** Carlos is sick today.
   B: He's sick?
   A: Yes, he's sick today. Write *sick*.
2. **B: cold.** Carmen has a cold.
   C: Who has a cold?
   B: Carmen has a cold. Write *cold*.
3. **C: fever.** Ali has a fever.
   D: You say he has a fever?
   C: Yes, Ali has a fever. Write *fever*.
4. **D: cough.** Hiroshi has a cough.
   A: Does Hiroshi have a cold or a cough?
   D: A cough. Write *cough*.
5. **A: sore throat.** Petra has a sore throat.
   B: You say Petra has a sore throat?
   A: Yes, that's right. Petra has a sore throat. Write *sore throat*.

Page 86 *What hurts?*
Listen and write.

1. **A: Back.** Van's back hurts.
   B: You say,"Van's back?"
   A: Yes, Van's back hurts. Write *back*.
2. **B: Head.** Rose's head hurts.
   C: Rose's hand or head?
   B: Rose's head hurts. Write *head*.
3. **C: Stomach.** Charlie's stomach hurts.
   D: You say, "Stomach?"
   C: Yes, s-t-o-m-a-c-h. Stomach. His stomach hurts. Write *stomach*.
4. **D: Knee.** Bic's knee hurts.
   A: Is it his knee?
   D: Yes, his knee, k-n-e-e. His knee hurts. Write *knee*.
5. **A: Ear.** Makeba's ear hurts.
   B: Her ear? e-a-r?
   A: Yes, her ear hurts. Write *ear*.
6. **B: tooth.** Pedro's tooth hurts.
   C: You say Pedro's tooth hurts?
   B: Yes, his tooth. t-o-o-t-h. His tooth hurts. Write *tooth*.

Page 87 *Listen.*
Listen and circle *yes* **or** *no.*

1. **A:** Does Ali have a fever?
   B: A fever?
   A: That's right. Does Ali have a fever? *yes*
2. **B:** Does Carmen's knee hurt?
   C: Knee?
   B: Yes, knee. Does Carmen's knee hurt? *no*

3. **C:** This is Makeba. Does her tooth hurt?
   D: Her tooth?
   C: Yep, does her tooth hurt? *no*
4. **D:** Do you see Bic? Does his knee hurt?
   A: Knee?
   D: Yeah, his knee. Does his knee hurt? *yes*
5. **A:** Is Carlos sick today?
   B: Is he sick?
   A: That's correct. Is Carlos sick today? *yes*
6. **B:** I think Van's back hurts. Does his back hurt?
   D: His back?
   B: Right, his back. Does his back hurt? *yes*
7. **D:** Charlie ate three hamburgers. Does his stomach hurt?
   A: Are you asking about his stomach?
   D: Yes, his stomach. Does his stomach hurt? *yes*
8. **A:** Petra is sick. Does her tooth hurt?
   B: Her tooth?
   A: Yes, her tooth. Does her tooth hurt? *no*
9. **B:** Does Hiroshi have a fever?
   C: A fever?
   B: Right, a fever. Does Hiroshi have a fever? *no*
10. **C:** Does Rose's head hurt?
    D: Rose's head?
    C: Yes, her head. Does Rose's head hurt? *yes*
11. **D:** Does Pedro's tooth hurt?
    A: His tooth?
    D: That's correct. His tooth. Does Pedro's tooth hurt? *yes*
12. **A:** Mr. Duval is sick. Does his throat hurt?
    B: Are you saying foot or throat ?
    A: I'm saying throat. Does his throat hurt? *yes*

Page 91 *Feeling better?*
Listen and read. What do you do to feel better when you have a cold?

1. **A: pills.** When we are sick, we often take pills. Read *pills*.
2. **B: aspirin.** Find the bottle of aspirin. Read *aspirin*.
3. **C: cough syrup.** Take cough syrup for a cough. Read *cough syrup*.
4. **D: cold medicine.** Take cold medicine for a cold. Read *cold medicine*.
5. **A: nose drops.** Take nose drops for a stuffy nose. Read *nose drops*.
6. **B: ear drops.** Use ear drops for an earache. Read *ear drops*.

Page 97   Grandpa wants to take the bus.
Listen and circle.

This is a bus pass.
Find the words *transit authority*. Circle *transit authority*—t-r-a-n-s-i-t a-u-t-h-o-r-i-t-y. Circle *transit authority*.

Talk with your teacher about the meaning.
Circle *good for one month*.
Talk with your teacher about the meaning.
Complete the date.
Talk with your teacher about the meaning.

Page 100   How do you come to school?
Listen and read.

1. **A:** Do you come to school by bicycle?
   B: By bicycle? Yes, by bicycle. Read *by bicycle*.
2. **B:** Do you come to school by motorcycle?
   C: By motorcycle? Yes, by motorcycle. Read *by motorcycle*.
3. **C:** Do you come to school by car?
   D: By car? Yes, by car. Read *by car*.
4. **D:** Do you come to school by train?
   A: By train? Yes, by train. Read *by train*.

5. **A:** Do you come to school on foot?
   B: On foot? Yes, on foot. Read *on foot*.
6. **A:** Do you come to school by bus?
   B: By bus? Yes, by bus. Read *by bus*.
7. **B:** Do you come to school by taxi?
   C: By taxi? Yes, by taxi. Read *by taxi*.
8. **C:** Do you come to school by subway?
   D: By subway? No, I never come by subway. Read *by subway*.

Page102   Grandpa's ride home on the bus.
Listen and write the words.

1. **drug store.** Grandpa buys cold medicine at the drug store. Write *drugstore*.
2. **laundromat.** Many students wash clothes at the laundromat. Write *laundromat*.
3. **gas station.** Bic fills his car at the gas station. Write *gas station*.
4. **restaurant.** The Apple family likes to eat at the Sea Siam Restaurant. Write *restaurant*.
5. **movie theater.** On Saturday night, Kim and May go to the movie theater. Write *movie theater*.
6. **bakery.** Mrs. Said likes to buy fresh bread at the bakery. Write *bakery*.

Page 111   Jobs, jobs, jobs.
Listen, read, and write.

1. **Alicia:** Hi! I'm Alicia. I'm a factory worker. Find my picture and write the name of my job. Write *factory worker*.
2. **Sue:** Hello, my name is Sue Apple. I'm a teacher. Find my picture and write the name of my job. Write *teacher*.
3. **Juan:** What's up? I'm Juan. I'm a security guard. Find my picture and write the name of my job. Write *security guard*.
4. **Ibrahim:** Hello, sir: May I help you? I'm Ibrahim, your food server. Find my picture and write the name of my job. Write *food server*.
5. **Carlos:** Hey there. You know me. I'm Carlos. I'm a construction worker. Find my picture. Write the name of my job. Write *construction worker*.
6. **Custodian:** Whew! I'm tired. I'm a custodian. Find my picture. Write the name of my job. Write *custodian*.
7. **Javier:** I'm a barber. Find my picture. Write the name of my job. Write *barber*.
8. **George:** Hello. It's me, George. My job is that of a secretary. Find my picture. Write the name of my job. Write *secretary*.
9. **Dominique:** Welcome. My name is Dominique. I'm a computer entry person. Find my picture. Write the name of my job. Write *computer entry person*.

10. **Therese:** Good afternoon. My name is Therese. I'm a nurse. Can you find my picture? Write the name of my job. Write *nurse*.
11. **Pedro:** Hi, I'm Pedro. I'm a gardener. Find my picture and write the name of my job. Write *gardener*.
12. **Makeba:** Hi, there. We've already met. I'm Makeba. I'm a manicurist. Find my picture. Write the name of my job. Write *manicurist*.

Page 113   Hire or fire.
Listen and read.

1. **on time.** Carlos is always on time. Read *on time*.
2. **late.** Poor Ms. Smith. Her word processor, Dominique, is always late. Read *late*.
3. **overtime.** Rose Ly works overtime a lot. Read *overtime*.
4. **vacation.** Do you get time off for vacation at your job? Read *vacation*.
5. **absent.** Don't be absent from your job too many times. Read *absent*.
6. **hire.** Jacques likes to hire good workers. Read *hire*.
7. **fire.** The boss must fire her for being late and absent too many times. Read *fire*.
8. **lay off.** The boss says, "Sorry no work." He must lay off the worker. Read *lay off*.

Page 122   Jack's office.
Listen and read.

1. **A: file cabinet.** Do you see the file cabinet?
   B: Yes, Grandpa is putting papers in the file cabinet.
   A: Read *file cabinet*.
2. **B: adding machine.** Find #2. This is the adding machine. Read *adding machine*.
3. **C: copier.** The copier is across from the telephone answering machine. Read *copier*.
4. **D: fax machine.** Find #4. The fax machine is between the typewriter and the computer. Read *fax machine*.
5. **A: calculator.** Do you see a *calculator*?
   B: Yes. The calculator is on the edge of the desk.
   A: Read *calculator*.
6. **B: telephone answering machine.** Find #6. The telephone answering machine is on the left side of the desk. Read *telephone answering machine*.
7. and 8. **C:** Find numbers 7 and 8. The **computer screen** is #7 and the **computer keyboard** is #8. Read *computer screen* and *computer key board*.
9. **D: waste basket.** Can you find the waste basket? Read *waste basket*.
10. **B: typewriter.** What about the typewriter? Where is it?
    A: The typewriter is next to the fax machine.
    B: Read *typewriter*.

Page 124   Review.
Listen, read, and write the letter.

1. The file cabinet is next to the door. Write the letter on the file cabinet. *H*
2. One wastebasket is between the fax machine and the file cabinet. Write the letter of the wastebasket. *D*
3. The adding machine is to the right of the computer. Write the letter of the adding machine. *A*
4. The telephone answering machine is on the table. Write the letter of the telephone answering machine. *F*
5. The computer is to the right of the calendar. *B*
6. The fax machine is to the left of the computer. *G*
7. The other wastebasket is under the table. *C*
8. The calculator is beside the answering machine. *E*

Page 125   Review.
Listen. Find the letters you hear.

Using the drawing of the computer, listen and touch these keys.
1. Find and touch *p*.
2. Find and touch *e*.
3. Find and touch *n*.
4. Find and touch *c*.
5. Find and touch *i*.
6. Find and touch *l*.
What word did you spell?
Work with your partner. Help each other spell other words by finding the letters on the computer keyboard.

Page 127   Let's be safe!
Listen and read.

A: a. Women. This sign says Women.
B: The Women's Room is here?
A: Yes, this is a Women's Room. Read **Women**.
D. b. Men. This sign tells us that there is a Men's Room near.

A: A Men's Room?
D: Yes, read **Men**.
A: c. Quiet. This sign says Quiet.
B: Sh-h-h?
A: Yes, be quiet. Read **Quiet**.
B: d. Keep out. This sign says Keep Out.
C: Do you mean stay away?
B: Yes, keep out. Read **Keep Out**.
C: e. Exit. This sign says Exit.
D: Can I go out here?
C: Yes, exit. Read **Exit**.
D: f. Phone. This signs says Phone.
A: Can I find a phone here?
D: Yes, there is a phone here. Read **Phone**.
B: g. Emergency Exit Only. This sign says Emergency Exit Only.
C: Does that mean we can go out here if there is trouble?
B: Yes, use this door to leave or exit when there is an emergency. Read **Emergency Exit Only.**
C: h. Caution. This sign says Caution.
D: Does that mean to be careful?
C: Yes, caution means to be careful. Read **Caution.**
D: i. Do Not Touch. This sign says Do Not Touch!
A: I know. That means, Do not put your hand on it.
D: That's right. Read **Do Not Touch!**
A: j. Danger. This sign says Danger.
B: Danger means big trouble, doesn't it?
A: Yes, when you see Danger, you must stay away. Read **Danger.**
B: k. Do Not Enter. This sign says Do Not Enter. Read **Do Not Enter.**
C: l. No Smoking. This sign says No Smoking. Read **No Smoking.**

Page 128   They're helping Dad at work.
Listen and read.

1. **A:** Jack is sending a fax.
   B: Jack is sending a fax?
   A: That's right. Read *Jack is sending a fax*.
2. **B:** Dominique is using the computer.
   C: You say she is using the computer?
   B: Yes. Read *Dominique is using the computer.*
3. **C:** Thérèse is typing a letter.
   D: Typing a letter?
   C: Correct. Read *Thérèse is typing a letter.*
4. **D:** Gigi is using the calculator.
   A: Gigi is using the calculator?
   D: Yep. Read *Gigi is using the calculator.*
5. **B:** George is talking on the telephone.
   C: George is talking on the telephone?
   B: Correct. Read *George is talking on the telephone.*
6. **A:** Grandpa Duval is filing papers.
   B: He's filing papers?
   A: Yeah. Read *Grandpa Duval is filing papers.*
7. **B:** Dominique is making copies.
   D: Dominique is making copies?
   B: Right. Read *Dominique is making copies.*
8. **C:** Grandpa Duval is emptying the wastebasket.
   D: You say he is emptying the wastebasket?
   C: Yes. Read *Grandpa Duval is emptying the wastebasket.*
9. **A:** Jack is using the clothes-pressing machine.

B: George is using the clothes-pressing machine?
A: Correct. Read *George is using the clothes-pressing machine.*

Page 134 *The roof is leaking.*
First listen and then listen again and read.

1. **A:** The roof is leaking.
   B: The roof is leaking?
   A: That's correct. The roof is leaking.
2. **B:** The window is cracked.
   C: You say the window is cracked?
   B: Right. The window is cracked.
3. **C:** The faucet is dripping.
   D: The faucet is dripping, too?
   C: Yeah, the faucet is dripping.
4. **D:** The toilet is overflowing.
   A: The toilet is overflowing?
   D: Yep, the toilet is overflowing.
5. **A:** The stove is broken.
   B: You say the stove is broken?
   A: The stove is broken.
6. **B:** The television isn't working.
   C: It isn't working?
   B: The television isn't working.

7. **C:** The heat isn't working.
   D: You say the heat isn't working?
   C: That's right. The heat isn't working.
8. **A:** The shower isn't working.
   B: The shower is broken, too?
   A: You got it right. The shower isn't working.
9. **D:** The refrigerator is leaking.
   A: It's leaking?
   D: You bet. The refrigerator is leaking.

Page 137 *Who fixes the problems?*
Listen and read.

1. **plumber.** The plumber fixes the faucet, the shower, and the toilet. Read *plumber.*
2. **repairperson.** The repairperson fixes the roof and the window. Read *repairperson.*
3. **electrician.** The electrician fixes the refrigerator, the stove, and the heat. Read *electrician.*
4. **TV repairperson.** The TV repairperson fixes the VCR and the television. Read *TV repairperson.*

Page 146 *Carlos goes to the bank.*
Listen and read.

1. **cash.**
   A: I need to get twenty-five dollars in cash.
   B: Twenty-five dollars in cash? Will two tens and a five be okay?
   A: Sure. Just so it's cash.
   Read *cash.*
2. **credit card.**
   B: Can I pay for this with my credit card?
   C: Sure. What credit card do you have?
   B: Here it is. Will you take this credit card?
   Read *credit card.*
3. **ATM machine.**
   C: Where is the nearest ATM machine?
   D: We have an ATM machine just outside on the corner.
   C: Oh, I see it.
   Read *ATM machine.*
4. **ATM card.**
   D: I can't find my ATM card.
   A: Do you have your ATM card in your pocket?
   D: Oh, here it is. It's in my wallet.
   Read *ATM card.*
5. **check.**
   A: Will you take a check?
   D: Sure, we'll always take a check with the proper ID.
   A: Let me write you a check.
   Read *check.*

6. **checking account**.
   B: Can I open a checking account?
   C: Yes. Will you open the checking account today?
   B: Yes, today is fine for me to open the checking account.
   Read *checking account.*
7. **money order.**
   C: I'd like to buy a money order.
   D: O.K. There is a charge of five dollars for a money order.
   C: Sure. Here's the five dollars for the money order.
   Read *money order.*

Page 149 *"Can I have a Change of Address form?"*
Listen and read.

1. **A:** **stamps.** Can I have a book of stamps?
   B: A book of stamps?
   A: Yes, that's right. A book of stamps, please.
   Read *stamps.*
2. **B:** **letter.** I need to mail a letter.
   C: Are you going to the post office to mail the letter?
   B: Yes, that's right. That's where I'll mail the letter.
   Read *letter.*
3. **C:** **package.** Can I send a package here?
   D: Of course, you can send the package here.
   C: How much to send the package?
   D: $6.50 to send the package.
   Read *package.*

4. **D:** **Change of Address form.** Can I have a
    Change of Address form?

   A: Yep. This is where you get the Change of Address
    form.

   D: How much for the Change of Address form?

   A: It's free. Read *Change of Address form.*

5. **B:** **post card.** How much for a post card?

   C: A post card? Just one post card?

   B: Yes, I want just one post card.
    Read *post card.*

6. **C:** **money order.** Can I buy a money order at the
    bank and at the post office?

   D: Yep, at both the bank and the post office you can
    buy a money order.

   C: Then, I'll buy a money order here.
    Read *money order.*

Underline the words you hear.

1. **package.** Underline #3, package. *package*
2. **stamps.** Underline #1, stamps. *stamps*
3. **Change of Address form.** Underline #4, Change of
   Address form. *Change of Address form.*
4. **money order.** Underline #6, money order. *Money
   order.*
5. **letter.** Underline #2, letter. Underline *letter.*
6. **post card.** Underline #5, post card. Underline *post
   card.*

STUDENT BOOK UNIT 14
TAPESCRIPT

Those kids!

Page 158   Are you angry? Are you pleased?
Listen and read.

   a. John is so angry. Read *angry.*
   b. But Kathy is so pleased. Read *pleased.*
   c. Sometimes Bic is lazy. Read *lazy.*
   d. But Juan is hard-working. Read *hard-working.*
   e. She's often dirty. Read *dirty.*
   f. She's always clean. Read *clean.*
   g. Gigi's room is so messy. Read *messy.*
   h. But, now, it is very, very neat. Read *neat.*
   i. Dominique is always late. Read *late.*
   j. Carlos is always early. Read *early.*
   k. The boy likes to run fast. Read *fast.*
   l. The old man likes to walk slow. Read *slow.*
   m. Frank can be so noisy. Read *noisy.*
   n. May is always quiet. Read *quiet.*
   o. She eats too little. Read *too little.*
   p. He eats too much. Read *too much.*

Underline the words you hear.

1. Underline *messy* and *neat.*
2. Underline *late* and *early.*
3. Underline *angry* and *pleased.*
4. Underline *fast* and *slow.*
5. Underline *too little* and *too much.*
6. Underline *dirty* and *clean.*
7. Underline *noisy* and *quiet.*
8. Underline *lazy* and *hard-working.*

Page 165 You kids!

**Listen and write the word under the correct
picture.**

   a. **short**. Her hair is very short. Read *short.*
   b. **long.** Her hair is so long. Read *long.*
   c. **small.** The blue car is very small. Read *small.*
   d. **large.** The red car is so large. Read *large.*
   e. **thin.** My brother is too thin. Read *thin.*
   f. **heavy.** Your brother is too heavy? Read *heavy.*
   g. **curly.** Her hair is curly. Read *curly.*
   h. **straight.** His hair is straight. Read *straight.*

Page 166 Kim likes makeup!

**Listen and write the word under the correct
picture.**

   a. **eyes.** Kim has beautiful eyes. *eyes*
   b. **neck.** Kim often wears a necklace on her neck. *neck*
   c. **mouth.** Kim wears lipstick on her mouth. *mouth*
   d. **eyelashes.** Kim likes to make her eyelashes black.
      eyelashes
   e. **eyebrow.** Our eyebrows are above our eyes.
      eyebrow
   f. **cheek.** Kim likes to make her cheeks pink. *cheek*
   g. **ear.** She wears earrings on her ears. *ear.*
   h. **teeth.** Look at her teeth. Her teeth are clean and
      white. *teeth*
   i. **nose.** She has a very nice nose. *nose*

Listen and read.

What foods do people take to parties?

1. **chips.** Potato chips, shrimp chips, tortilla chips. Chips everywhere. Read *chips*.
2. **juice.** Orange juice, papaya juice, grape juice. Great juice. Read *juice*.
3. **tortillas.** Great tacos are made from tortillas. Read *tortillas*.
4. **salsa.** Chips and tortillas need great salsa. Read *salsa*.
5. **egg rolls.** I like shrimp and pork egg rolls. Read *egg rolls*.
6. **sushi.** Will you bring the sushi? Read *sushi*.
7. **pita bread.** Can you eat a pita? Read *pita bread*.
8. **hot dogs.** I like onions on my hot dogs. Read *hot dogs*.
9. **pizza.** Pizza. Pizza. Pizza pie. Read *pizza*.
10. **salad.** Everyone loves salad. Read *salad*.
11. **meat and rice.** Almost everyone loves meat and rice. Read *meat and rice*.
12. **sandwiches.** Americans love sandwiches. Read *sandwiches*.

Listen and underline the words you hear.

Meat and rice. Almost everyone loves meat and rice. Underline *meat and rice*.

Hot dogs. I like onions on my hot dogs. Underline *hot dogs*.

Potato chips, shrimp chips, tortilla chips. Chips everywhere. Underline *chips*.

Pita bread. Can you eat a pita? Underline *pita bread*.

Sandwiches. Americans love sandwiches. Underline *sandwiches*.

Pizza. Pizza. Pizza. Pizza pie. Underline *pizza*.

Egg rolls. I like shrimp and pork egg rolls. Underline *egg rolls*.

Salad. Everyone loves salad. Underline *salad*.

Juice. Orange juice, papaya juice, grape juice. Great juice. Underline *juice*.

Tortillas. Great tacos are made from tortillas. Underline *tortillas*.

Sushi. Will you bring the sushi? Underline *sushi*.

Listen and write.

Grandpa is getting ready for the party. He is taking a shower and brushing his teeth, and he is shaving. He is getting dressed and combing his hair. When he is ready, he takes his food for the potluck, reads his map to the party, and walks to the bus stop.